GRIEVING *FORWARD*

DEATH
HAPPENED
NOW WHAT?

GRIEVING FORWARD

DEATH HAPPENED NOW WHAT?

A Practical Guide for
Healing & Understanding
the Grief Process

CATHY CLOUGH & LINDA POULIOT

REDEMPTION PRESS

ISBN: 978-1-68314-350-5

This book is dedicated to you, dear friend.
We are sorry your loved one has died.
We hear your cries of sorrow;
we acknowledge your grief and pain.

Our prayer for you is healing.
Please accept the gift of hope and healing
which is wrapped in love throughout
each and every page of this book.

Even though it seems impossible right now,
healing is possible.

Allow the information in this book to support,
guide, and encourage you as you journey along
the path of grief, all the way to the destination
of healing, acceptance, and new beginnings.

ACKNOWLEDGMENTS

A note from Cathy:

I would like to thank Mary Lindquist, the hospice nurse who helped my family when my first husband Don was dying. Mary saw something in me that I did not see and hired me to start a bereavement program at Arbor Hospice and Home Care. Because of the door that Mary opened for me, fourteen years later, I was able to take a "leap of faith" and establish New Hope Center for Grief Support, a non-profit, Christian based grief support center.

I would also like to thank John and Betty Baird, who made it possible for New Hope Center for Grief Support to become a reality. Thank you, John and Betty, for your continued support, friendship and prayers for the ministry of New Hope.

I've been privileged to help grieving people for over twenty-five years, but I still learn something new from each person going through their own individual grief experience. A special thanks to all of my dear friends who have attended New Hope Center for Grief Support groups, workshops, and on-going groups. Living the grief process has made you the "real" experts and teachers in this field.

I also want to thank the individual supporters, churches, funeral homes and private businesses that sponsor our workshops and on-going groups. And, a very special thanks to all of our many volunteers, facilitator's and workshop speakers.

God has placed a special anointing on this ministry. Thank you to our "Team Leader," God, for opening the doors for us to minister to those who have experienced the death of a loved one.

A note from Linda:

My first thank you is to Cathy Clough. The information that I learned in my eight week From Grief to New Hope workshop at my church, shortly after Donald died, positively changed the direction of my healing and my life. I was also able to use this same information to help my children heal. Thank you for taking the "leap of faith" and founding New Hope Center for Grief Support. I am forever grateful.

I would also like to thank Nancy Stoner. I have learned so much from you while co-facilitating From Grief to New Hope support groups over the last eight years. Your knowledge and wisdom are woven into every written word on each page of this book. You are a gifted teacher, mentor and my very special friend.

Last, but not least, I would like to thank my dear friend, Mary Hayek. Shortly after my first husband Donald died, Mary showed up in my life and took me by the hand. As she walked the path of grief with me, she taught me everything that she had learned while "living" through the grief process herself after the death of her husband, Tom. Mary also explained to me that it was my responsibility and my duty to take someone else that is grieving by the hand and walk the path with them...and soon after planting that seed in my heart, the idea for this book was born. Thank you, Mary.

TABLE OF
CONTENTS

PITFALLS AND POTHOLES ALONG THE PATH

THE BELONGINGS

ANGER

DEALING WITH FEELINGS

SPECIAL DAYS AND HOLIDAYS

FINDING A "NEW NORMAL"

INTRODUCTION: UNDERSTANDING "THE GRIEF PROCESS"

What is happening to me? What happens next? Information is the remedy for eliminating the uneasiness that comes with not knowing what the future holds and the fear that many times clings to a griever's heart, mind, and soul after experiencing the death of a close loved one. The grief process, like any other process in life, can be learned. The grief process is a journey.

We have found it helpful to visualize the grief journey as a path or road that we follow. Similar to any other path or road, this one has twists, turns, bumps, pitfalls, and potholes which need to be navigated. As a result of all the twists, turns, bumps, pitfalls, and potholes, we sometimes feel as if we have taken two steps forward followed by what seems like three enormous steps backward. From experience, we also know that no path or road is exactly the same. And just like any other path or road, this one has a destination. The destination in this case is healing, acceptance, and new beginnings.

It was not your choice to travel down the path of grief. But you do have a choice in how you respond to this challenge. Choose healing. Allow the information in this book to guide you as you navigate the path of grief. In the beginning, this means just putting one foot in front of the other, getting through the day, and if you have children, remembering to feed both them and yourself.

The following is an overview of the different phases of grief that you will cycle through (sometimes more than once, and many times phases overlap) as you heal. It may be helpful to look at these phases as road markers along the path of grief. Remember, too: the choices that you make as you journey along this path will determine the direction that you take and the outcome.

THE PATH OF GRIEF

Numbness

Many of us remember watching President Kennedy's wife, Jackie Kennedy (Onassis) on television after the president was assassinated. During her husband's funeral, she maintained a stoic, almost "too together" appearance. She was numb and in shock. As someone in one New Hope Center for Grief support group once said, "Numb is good." If the death of a loved one was sudden and unexpected, the first thoughts, whether verbalized or not verbalized, are usually, "No this can't be true—not him/her!" This usually leads to numbness—the time when you can put on a front and get through the early days and the funeral. You haven't yet begun to deal with the reality of the loss. Did it really happen?

What you can do: Be thankful for the numbness. Since the numbness is short-lived, allow people who offer you support and comfort to be there for you. You may not feel the need for them now, but you will, and you'll want them to be available.

Pain

It happened and it hurts. You realize it but can't believe it yet. The tears start coming, and you wonder if you'll ever be able to function normally again. There is an ache in your chest that you just can't seem to get rid of. You welcome sleep, since this is the only time you're not in pain. This is a time when you may want to stay in bed and pull the covers over your head. What's the point in getting up if he/she is not there? Some people choose to run during this time and keep busy, busy, busy, believing that if they are busy, they won't have to feel the pain as much.

What you can do: Allow yourself to feel the pain even though it hurts. When you begin to think about the person who died, think the thoughts completely through even though doing so may cause you to cry. Remember, tears are healing. Plan something that will *make you* get up in the morning. Try to find a balance between staying at home and getting out so that you can allow yourself time to grieve while still getting out among people. If you choose to be on the go all the time, you won't be able to take the time to grieve. The grief will eventually catch you, so you might as well deal with it now while the world expects you to be grieving.

Disorientation

You may find yourself losing your temper at unusual times and places. You may feel restless and find yourself pacing, not knowing whether you're coming or going. You may start things you cannot finish, misplace things you cannot find. You may feel as if you are losing your mind. This can cause frustration, and you don't know where to turn.

What you can do: Get involved in a grief support group. There are two major benefits for participating in grief support groups. First, it will help you normalize your grief responses so that you will realize you are not, in fact, losing your mind—you're grieving! Secondly, you will meet others who understand and who will allow you to grieve and act a little crazy sometimes. Your family and other friends who haven't "been there" may not understand. Find ways to work through the frustrations you are feeling. For example, exercise is a good stress releaser. Take care of yourself.

Realization

It hits you now. The person who died is never coming back and the finality of death becomes very clear. You may feel that life is not worth living. How can you possibly go on without that person in your life? You may feel that there is no future for you. How could there be when the person you loved so deeply is gone, never to return? During this time, you may feel intense anger and find yourself lashing out at people for no apparent reason. You may feel strong feelings of guilt, recognized by using terms such as "If only" or "I should have" a lot when referring to the deceased person. You may find that you begin self-blaming, and because of this feeling, become angry at yourself, even hating yourself and feeling as if you don't deserve a future.

What you can do: It is important to tell yourself that all of these feelings are normal; by completing the grief process you will get to a place where you will choose to go on and make a new life and future. Many people can't imagine this at the time, but you have to hold on to that fact. During this time, we need to deal with our intense emotions—the anger, the guilt, the lack of self-worth. Talking about these feelings, dealing with them completely, and eventually letting them go should be our goal.

Readjustment

You've come to a place where you realize that you can go on and begin the process of making a new life for yourself. You begin to smile again, sometimes feeling guilty when you do. You've been able to let go of the self-blame and the anger and have taken steps to begin anew, striving to find a "New Normal." This is the time many people feel a need to find meaning in the death and some begin their search with a new or renewed relationship with God. You begin to think realistically about the person who died and realize that you will always miss the person and remember him/her with love, but you can and will make a life without that person. You have to. You may feel surges of guilt when you think those thoughts, but that's normal, too.

What you can do: Begin to set some goals. Choose to refuse to take back the anger and the guilt feelings associated with your grief. Think positive thoughts. Begin to plan for a future. Make some changes in your life. Look at yourself—your inner and outer self and make any improvements you can which will help you feel better about yourself and prepare you for this new life. This would be a good time to seek God's guidance and allow him to help you.

Reestablishment

You have re-entered the world once again. You will never be the same—you are forever changed. But, life is worth living again. This is the time when you'll choose to place the person who died and the memories associated with that person in a special place in your heart—a place where you can find him/her whenever you choose to. You will choose to establish new, close relationships, maybe even reestablish relationships with people you moved away from in your early grief period.

What you can do: Act on the goals you've set. Use the tremendous loss you have experienced to help others. Make some positive changes in your life. Allow yourself to be happy and content and at peace with where you have been and where you are going.

Grief Work Is Hard Work

In his book *The Developing Mind,* author Daniel Siegel explains how hard your body and mind are working:

> In the case of the death of a loved one, the mind is forced to alter the structure of its internal working models to adjust to the painful reality that you can no longer seek proximity and gain comfort from your loved one. Every part of your body and mind are adjusting to accepting the reality of the death. You are working through the pain of grief, adjusting to an environment in which the deceased person is missing, emotionally relocating the deceased person, all with the long-range goal of somehow moving on with your life. [1]

The Five Needs of Every Griever

Grief expert Victoria Alexander identified the first three needs of every griever: "finding the words of an unimaginable loss, speaking them out loud, and knowing that they have been heard."[2] These three elements are critical for healing, but there are two more needs that all grievers share. Each griever needs to learn about the grief process. Each griever also needs to do the work of grief—his or her personal grief work. [3]

Please speak the following words aloud. I need to:

Put words to my feelings of grief
Speak those words aloud
Know that I have been heard
Learn about the grief process
Do my personal grief work

The Payoff Is Healing

Grief work is probably the hardest work you will ever do. The payoff is healing. Healing does not mean forgetting your loved one. Healing does not mean that you need to stop loving your loved one either or that you no longer miss your loved one.

Doing the work of grief allows you to return to a place of wholeness and normal functioning again. Helping you navigate your journey down the path of grief is our hearts' desire. We are holding out our hands to you. Grab on! We will walk side-by-side with you as you journey along the path.

Sincerely,
Cathy and Linda

THANK GOD FOR NUMB

FINDING THE WORDS I NEED

Before them the earth shakes, the sky trembles, the sun and moon are darkened, and the stars no longer shine.

(Joel 2:10, Compton's Interactive NIV)

This verse refers to an astounding invasion of locusts that went on for days. It has been described as a "living deluge" that seemed like it was never going to end. The locusts destroyed everything in their path. Sounds a lot like the invasion and impact of grief—don't you think?

You felt the deluge of grief rip through your body, mind, heart, and soul with a crushing and lacerating raw energy and pain. Your entire being shook and vibrated from the impact. You felt your heart tremble and break into a million pieces. Emotions that were once comfortable together exploded into uncomfortable, painful chaos. The veil of grief darkened the world, the sun, and moon. The stars now appear to no longer shine. And the pain feels like it truly is N-E-V-E-R going to end.

Even though this is a fairly accurate description of what the impact of grief feels like, death teaches that there is not one word or group of words in any language that even comes close to describing what the lacerating sting of death and the pain of grief truly feel like. However, what we need to remember is that words are still helpful "healing tools." It's through the use of words that we process, comprehend, assimilate, and slowly make sense out of what has happened not only to our loved one or loved ones, *but to us!* Putting words to our feelings enables each of us to name, claim, and sort out what we are feeling. The problem for many of us is this: the death related numbness that we experience physically and emotionally after a death, many times impacts our ability to come up with words that are descriptive of what we are feeling. You are not alone if you feel as if your brain has been emptied of all words.

This numbness, which impacts each griever, is actually a gift of protection—compliments of God. He designed us with this feature because we need to be insulated from the pain after the death of a loved one. In fact, the impact of the loss without the benefits of emotional numbness would probably overwhelm most of us. Eventually, the numbness begins to melt away and we miss it.

Even if you are not having a problem finding words, this exercise will provide you with even more expressive "healing tools." Find yourself on the following list.[3] Check off the words that describe what you are feeling. Claim each word by speaking it aloud. Sometimes it is helpful to write each word down on paper, too.

Words that describe grief:

☐ Affliction   ☐ Mourning

☐ Agony   ☐ Pain

☐ Anguish   ☐ Regret

☐ Bereavement   ☐ Remorse

☐ Burden   ☐ Sadness

☐ Dejection   ☐ Sorrow

☐ Desolation   ☐ Suffering

☐ Distress   ☐ Tragedy

☐ Grievance   ☐ Trial

☐ Heartache   ☐ Tribulation

☐ Heartbreak   ☐ Trouble

☐ Misery   ☐ Woe

A definition of grief: *Merriam Webster's Collegiate Dictionary* says that grief is the "deep and poignant distress caused by or as if by bereavement, sorrow." It goes on to state that sorrow means "deep distress, sadness, or regret especially for the loss of something or someone loved." [4]

Grief, my friend, is the expected, *normal* reaction to each loss that we experience during our lifetime. We all experience loss of youth and all the different losses that come with aging. Some of us experience loss of health. Sometimes we experience loss of employment or sadly a divorce. Many times, we experience multiple losses in a short period of time, complicating grief. We need to grieve each loss that we experience.

A Gem of Hope:

The sun, moon and stars will eventually shine again for you. Cling to this promise as you find healing words that propel you forward, one baby step at a time, along the path of grief.

The Destination Is Healing: Action Step

Pick out words from the list that describe and express what you are feeling. Write the words down. Speak the words aloud.

COMMON RESPONSES
TO GRIEF

I have no peace, no quietness; I have no rest, but
only turmoil.

(Job 3:26)

No peace, no quietness, no rest...well, no wonder! Every
cell in your body is working through the raw pain of grief.
Emotions that once operated in a comfortable and familiar
pattern are now functioning in a state of anarchy. Nothing
makes any sense; self esteem wanes, and the tidal waves of
fear that often accompany grief are capable of ravaging the
strongest soul.

After a death, the brain is also in the process of tack-
ling a huge job. The brain must "rewire" to a new environment that does not include the deceased.[5] At the same
time, the deepest yearning screaming from our brains and
hearts is to have our loved one back. We desperately want
to return to the safety and comfort of life as we knew and
understood it—before the death happened. During this
period of "rewiring" and turmoil, it is normal for a griever
to experience many different emotional and physical
responses. We need to put words to these responses, too.

Please find yourself on the following list. Check off or
make a mental note of which reactions you are experienc-

ing. You may have a few responses of your own to add to the list.

Hospice of Michigan-Reactions to Grief:[6]

(www.hospiceofmichigangriefreactions)

PHYSICAL AND MENTAL REACTIONS

☐ SLEEP DISTURBANCES/DREAMS

☐ WEIGHT AND APPETITE CHANGES

☐ WEAKNESS AND FATIGUE

☐ DEEP SIGHING

☐ DECREASED RESISTANCE TO ILLNESS

☐ RESTLESSNESS/IMPATIENCE

☐ RAPID HEART BEAT

☐ INCREASED BLOOD PRESSURE

☐ TIGHTNESS IN CHEST

☐ DIFFICULTY SWALLOWING

☐ PIT IN STOMACH

- [ ] Decision-making impaired

- [ ] Concentration difficulties

- [ ] Forgetfulness

- [ ] Crying

Behavioral Reactions

- [ ] Preoccupation

- [ ] Apathy regarding activities

- [ ] Decreased activity

- [ ] Detachment from surroundings

- [ ] Disorientation to time and place

- [ ] Withdrawal from friends

- [ ] Seeking solitude

Emotional Reactions

- [ ] Shock

- [ ] Disbelief

- [ ] Numbness

- ☐ Confusion

- ☐ Sadness/depression

- ☐ Guilt

- ☐ Yearning/loneliness

- ☐ Fears/anxiety

- ☐ Feeling of being lost

- ☐ Anger

Spiritual Reactions

- ☐ Reevaluation of beliefs

- ☐ Anger at God

- ☐ Distance/closeness with God

- ☐ Difficulty attending place of worship

Forgetting to pay bills, feed yourself, feed your children, and losing keys are all normal when someone is grieving. So are having panic attacks or experiencing the same symptoms that your loved one experienced while he or she was in the process of dying. Dizziness and muscular tension are also common.

Sometimes, we experience different responses one time or only a few times. But most people rotate through whatever different responses they are experiencing many times. Do we all experience the same responses? No. Does everyone grieve the same? No. Each of us has his or her own individual way (healthy/productive or not) of dealing with stress, problem solving, perceiving, and expressing. Each of us has also had a different life experience and each of us has had a different death experience. It's also important to remember that each person's relationship with his or her loved one was unique. The relationship that you had with your loved one will impact your responses.[7]

Most life-event scales that are used to measure stress levels list the death of a spouse as the number one stressor in life. The death of a close family member follows. The bottom line for you is that your loved one has died and this death *is* your number one life stressor (physical and emotional) right now. Multiple deaths complicate the stress response.

Because you are physically and emotionally functioning under the highest possible level of stress, this is not the time to take any chances with your health or to make any assumptions regarding different responses or symptoms that you are experiencing. Now is the time to go over all your responses and symptoms with your physician.

Many grievers experience high blood pressure for the first time after a death. High blood pressure is known as "the Silent Killer." You won't know if you have developed high blood pressure unless you get checked. Make your appointment today. Your loved one would want you to. We want you to. You need you to.

A Gem of Hope:

Peace, quietness, and rest do slowly return. Early in grief, it is difficult for most grievers to sleep. Many times the ability to sleep is impacted negatively by dehydration from sweating and crying. You can positively impact your ability to sleep by drinking plain water and rehydrating.

The Destination Is Healing: Action Step

Movement and fresh air are stress relieving and healing. Take a daily walk. Walking to the mail box counts—but eventually you will need to add more steps to your walk. Try adding a few steps each day. If you don't have sidewalks, head to the mall or check for available walking times at your local high school.

FACTORS THAT IMPACT GRIEF

The LORD my God holds my right hand; He is the
LORD, Who says to me, Fear not; I will help you!

(Isaiah 41:13, AMP)

"Who" died is the first relationship factor impacting your
grief. Who died?

☐	SPOUSE	☐	PARTNER
☐	FIANCÉ(E)	☐	FAMILY MEMBER
☐	CHILD	☐	FRIEND
☐	SIBLING	☐	EX-SPOUSE
☐	PARENT	☐	OTHER: _____

There are also many other factors that impact and influence grief. And even though no one factor is more important than another, each factor has the potential to complicate grief or cause a person's grief to last longer. Some

factors automatically put a person at higher risk of complicated grief, just because of what they are. You need to put words to each factor that is impacting your grief. Please identify your personal factors.

Factors that impact grief:

☐ Sudden death

☐ Violent death-murder

☐ Anticipated death

☐ Suicide

☐ Parenting grieving children, teenagers or young adults

☐ Pregnant at the time of your spouse's death

☐ Your spouse was pregnant at the time of her death

☐ Multiple deaths/losses

☐ Exhaustion from care giving

☐ Your financial situation

☐ Your age

- [ ] Your cultural background

- [ ] Your physical/emotional health at the time of the death

- [ ] Survivor with grown children/step-children

- [ ] Survivor without children

- [ ] Auto accident/motorcycle accident

- [ ] Drug/alcohol related death

- [ ] Multiple grievers living/ working under one roof

- [ ] Good support system/lack of support system

- [ ] Close relationship with your loved one

- [ ] Poor relationship with loved one

- [ ] Unresolved issues stemming from past losses (death, divorce, job, abortion, death of a pet, etc.)

- [ ] When there is no body

- [ ] Unknown etiology

☐ RESOLVED ISSUES RELATED TO A PREVIOUS
LOSS OR DEATH THAT RESURFACE AND NEED
TO BE READDRESSED AGAIN AT THIS TIME

☐ UNKNOWN INFORMATION/SECRETS REGARDING
YOUR LOVED ONE THAT WERE REVEALED DURING
THEIR ILLNESS, DYING PROCESS, OR AFTER THEIR
DEATH

☐ YOUR PERSONAL UNIQUE WAY OF PROBLEM
SOLVING/DEALING WITH STRESS

Take a minute and review each box that you checked off. Part of healing is being honest about what we are dealing with. Let's take a closer look at some factors that automatically put a griever at a higher risk of complicated grief:

- Loss of Child: This includes miscarriage or stillborn child. It's not natural for a child to die before a parent. The death of a child is also the death of each parent's hopes, dreams, and expectations for that child. Many times, the parent's grief is further complicated by the necessity of tending to the needs of grieving siblings, family members and friends of the child.

- Sudden Death: The lack of time to prepare due to the unexpected suddenness of the death affects the griever's ability to cope and adapt. Any sense of control we thought we had over our life seems to vanish. An unexpected death leaves the griever with the extra complication of extreme shock, which is profound, confusing, and exhausting. It may take a few days or even a few weeks to accept the fact the death has actually occurred, even when we understand intellectually the death did occur. *Note: An anticipated death sometimes has the same impact as a sudden death if the death did not occur in the way we expected it to and/or when we expected it to. Problems occur when friends and/or family think that we should have been more prepared for the death than we actually were. The fact is, it is not the length of time that your loved one was dying that determines whether the death was sudden or anticipated. Your personal perception and the unique circumstances surrounding the death decide that.*

- Multiple Deaths: Each death must be grieved individually. Some people grieve one death at a time. Others rotate or process a little bit of grief from each death at a time until the grief involved with each death is resolved.

- Violent Death: A violent death is an unexpected, needless and brutal death. Murder, suicide, death due to terrorist attack or other act of war all fall under this category. The extra burden of dealing with the courts, media, etc., impacts both the grief process and the healing process.

- Suicide/AIDS/Drug Overdose—Stigma: Some types of death have a stigma attached to them. The most common are death by suicide, AIDS and drug overdose. When stigma is attached to a death either by others or by our own feelings of shame and embarrassment, the tendency is not to talk about our grief at all or if we do—without any honesty. When this happens we can get stuck in our grief. Grief counseling for the entire family is beneficial.

- Young Widowed Person: There are many unique and exhausting challenges that must be faced by younger widows and widowers. Let's identify a few:
    - Helping children grieve—this adds to the exhaustion you are already experiencing.
    - Learning to parent alone.
    - Feeling like nobody understands. Most younger widowed people don't know another young widowed person.
    - Financial problems. Often times there is no life insurance or pension.
    - In-law problems.
    - Loss of old friends.
    - Desire for opposite sex relationships— even remarriage.
    - For some, mourning the fact that they put off beginning their family.

- Parenting Grieving Children, Teenagers or Young Adults: Children grieve. It is difficult and exhausting to parent grieving children and deal with your own grief at the same time. A grieving parent needs to continue to engage emotionally, in a healthy manner, and to continue to parent in a healthy manner. This is hard parenting grief work after a death when the normal tendency is to focus on self. Sharing feelings is necessary and healing for children. Give each child the opportunity to share the words of his or her grief. Listen so that they know that the words of their grief have been heard. It is also normal to forget to feed children when we are grieving. Remember to feed your children.

- Personality Type of Griever: The "lens" which we view life through impacts us. Do you normally have a positive outlook? Or do you normally have a negative outlook? Do you view the glass as half empty or half full? We realize that many times it's hard to even find "the glass" right now. However, even when we are grieving it's important to understand that perception influences healing either positively or negatively.

A Gem of Hope:

Amid all these things I am more than a conqueror and gain surpassing victory through Him who loved me.

(Romans 8:37, AMP)

The Destination Is
Healing: Action Step

Identify the factors that are impacting you. Identify factors
that are impacting each of your children.

_____

_____

_____

_____

_____

_____

_____

_____

_____

_____

_____

_____

_____

_____

_____

_____

_____

_____

_____

WHAT NORMAL GRIEF IS NOT

If my heart is broken, I'll find God right there;
if I'm kicked in the gut, He'll help me catch my
breath.

(Psalms 34:18, MSG)

Since grief is the normal response to death, it would be
abnormal not to grieve. Your past, your loved one, and the
life that you created/shared together are a part of your personal history, your family history, and who you are. Sometimes when we are overwhelmed with the emotion of grief,
we try to deny our grief. Understanding what normal grief
is *not* frees us to move forward and heal. Let's take a look.

NORMAL GRIEF IS NOT:

- A sickness or a psychological illness: A statement we
  frequently hear is, "I feel like I am losing my mind."
  You are not alone. This is a common response. Normal
  grief itself is not a sickness or a psychological illness.
  However, it does feel like it sometimes for some of us.
  If you are concerned that you really are or could be
  losing your mind, make an appointment with a profes-

sional and get yourself checked out. Peace of mind is also an important component of healing.

- A sign of weakness: Allowing yourself to grieve is actually a sign of great strength. The raw painful energy and the brutal force of grief is what transports and pushes each of us through the piercing pain of grief toward healing.

- Something time alone heals: Unfortunately, the passing of time alone is not what heals. Learning about the grief process and doing the work of grief is what heals.

- Something you "get over" in a week or a month or a year: Even though some people think that we ought to, it is not humanly possible to just "get over" the death of a loved one. There is no magic time frame for returning to a place of normal functioning, either. Based on our own personal experience and what we have consistently observed over the years, it's not unusual for this process to take anywhere from two to five years. This information is not provided to scare you or to make you think that you're going to feel the way you do right now for two to five years. The physical symptoms go away and the emotional symptoms will lessen. You won't be crying on a regular basis. But to get to a place of normal functioning, functioning at the level you were at before your loved one died, takes a while.

- Something you can make yourself fast forward through because you want to be freed from the pain: Everyone tries, but nobody has figured out a way to accomplish this...and that's because it's not possible.

• Something that will go away if you self medicate with recreational/prescription drugs, alcohol, sex, food or excessive spending: Prescription drugs are necessary and helpful in some cases. However, drugs need to be taken as directed by and under the care of a physician. If you choose to numb your pain with drugs or alcohol to the point where you are not able to function, you need to understand that when you discontinue using, you will be starting your grief work at the point you were at when you started using. In other words, numbing the pain does not eliminate the need to do grief work. In addition, many people don't realize that alcohol is a depressant. If you have a history of drug and/or alcohol addiction in the past, relapsing now is possible for some people. For some people, food becomes the drug of choice. Emotional eating is a hard habit to break. Make the choice not to over-eat. Reward yourself with healthy, balanced and healing food. Try replacing over-eating with walking, running or biking. This is also not the time to jump into a sexual relationship. A new partner or multiple partners will not eliminate the pain of grief. This is high risk behavior that many times results in a sexually transmitted disease. The high from sex can be addicting, but only in the moment. Your heart is broken. You need to heal. For more information on sexually transmitted illness: www.cdc.gov/std/general

Finally, do not go on an excessive spending spree or loan money to anyone—including family members. You might need every penny you have to live on one day, even if you don't think you will right now. Spending money or giving it away will not fill up the hole in your heart either. Sometimes the act of spending or giving away money is really an attempt to purge guilt feelings which are being experienced because of how the money was acquired. For instance, receiving life insurance money triggers over-spending and/or giving money away for some people.

- Something that will go away if you find a new love interest: If your spouse or partner has died, a new love interest will not make the pain go away or eliminate the need to do grief work. Protect your heart from another loss. Dating and/or another relationship may be in your future, but not right now while you're not thinking straight. Unresolved grief will only contaminate a new relationship. Wait at least a year (two is even better) before you consider dating. It is important to live through all four seasons and experience every first special day (birthday, anniversary, each holiday, etc.) without your spouse or partner, including the first anniversary of the death.

- Something that moves predictably from one stage to the next: Again, most people find it helpful to visualize grief as a journey down a road or a path. When we think about a road or path, we think about all the twists and turns in the road, the bumps and potholes. No path or road is exactly the same. And sometimes, it's ten steps forward...and other times, it is ten steps backwards. But one thing every road or path has is an ending—a destination. When we are traveling down the path of grief, the destination we are heading for is healing, acceptance, and new beginnings.

- A sign of lack of faith: Job is the first person in the Bible that many people think of when they think about someone who experienced a long season of endless grief and suffering. His grief journey is recorded in the Old Testament in the book of Job. In Job 1:1, we learn that Job lived in the land of Uz, and that he was blameless, upright, and wealthy. Later in the first chapter, we read that fire (lightning) fell out of the sky and burned up his sheep and servants. Then, Chaldeans swept down out of the hills, carried off his camels, and murdered more of his servants. A short time later in a different location, the Sabeans attacked and murdered Job's remaining servants and rode off with his oxen and donkeys. Every time Job turned around, another messenger showed up with devastating news. Before Job even had time to comprehend all this horrible news, he was informed a greater tragedy had taken place. All his children were dead. A mighty wind had swept in from the desert and collapsed the house that they were in. Incredibly, when it seemed like it could not get any worse for Job, it did. He found himself covered with painful oozing sores from the top of his head to the bottom of his feet. Job shares his feelings of grief:

If only my anguish could be weighed and all my misery placed on scales! It would surely outweigh the sand of the sea.

(Job 6:2–3)

As we follow Job's journey, we learn through his dialogue with God that having a strong faith in God does not eliminate the emotional pain of grief. We also learn that it's okay to question God because Job did. This means, asking God why and outwardly expressing grief is not an indication we have a spiritual problem, or that there is something wrong with our relationship with God. Through Job's story, we come to understand that faith in God is the source of strength, comfort, and hope. Faith is what supports us as we walk through grief related fear, pain, loneliness, despair and anger.

A Gem of Hope:

Ask God for clarity, direction, and courage. He will help you catch your breath as you travel down the path of grief.

The Destination Is
Healing: Action Step

Write down (or just think about) what you learned about
what normal grief is not that surprised you?

_____

_____

_____

_____

_____

_____

_____

_____

_____

_____

_____

_____

_____

_____

_____

_____

_____

_____

_____

_____

NAVIGATING THE PATH OF GRIEF

THE NEED TO SPEAK MY WORDS OF GRIEF OUT LOUD

Research of various sorts in psychology and in neuroscience has revealed the important finding that people who use words to describe their internal states, such as their emotions and what they perceive, are more flexible and capable of regulating their emotions in a more adaptive manner.[8]

The Mindful Brain by Daniel J. Siegel

Every time you tell your story aloud your brain and heart are hearing the words again, too. If you really think about it, grievers need to hear their own stories in their own words, in their own voice, over and over again. Doing this helps your brain and heart comprehend the fact that the death really has occurred. In other words, we each need to hear our story over and over again to believe it!

Talking out loud helps us to sort out our emotions, opinions, and thoughts. Talking out loud also gives us the opportunity to process our experiences and gauge our progress. For instance, continually repeating the same negative words over and over again, without resolution, clues us in to the possibility that we are emotionally stuck. The thoughts that we think and words that we speak influence healing either positively or negatively.

In her book *Who Switched Off My Brain,* Dr. Caroline Leaf explains the relationship between what we think and the power contained within the words that we speak. She shares:

> "Thoughts stimulate emotions which then result in attitude and finally produce behavior...The words you speak are electromagnetic life forces that come from a thought inside your brain and are influenced by your five senses. They contain power and work hand-in-hand with your thought life, influencing the world around you and the circumstances of your thought life."[9]

The grief energy that you feel swirling in the core of your being is also consuming your emotions and thoughts. This energy needs to be released. Speaking the words of our grief is one avenue of release. Along with each word or "electromagnetic life force" which is spoken, a little bit of emotional grief energy is also released. Sharing our feelings with words also releases us from normal energy draining, grief-related thoughts. It's important to tell your story to anyone and everyone who will listen. Talking is an emotional release. Talk!

Strangers sometimes listen better and are more attentive than family members and friends. We forget sometimes family members and friends are also grieving. They need to tell their story and to be heard, too. It is easy to wear them out with the words of our story. This is why it is very beneficial to find new people with whom to share your story.

Tell your story to every telemarketer who calls. Tell every sales person and cashier that waits on you. When you find yourself waiting in a line, share your story with others who are also waiting in the line. Everywhere you go, tell people about your loved one.

God allows us to meet people who also need to talk about a deceased loved one and who need to be heard. We have noticed that path-crossing is a common occurrence among grievers. Many times when we exchange stories and *listen* to each other, friendship begins. Speak the words of your story. Listen as others share their words of grief.

A Gem of Hope:

Animals are excellent listeners. If you own a pet, take the time to walk, talk, and heal together. (Pets grieve, too.) If you live alone and don't own a pet, it may be time to consider adopting a furry friend. The local shelter is an excellent place to start your search.

The Destination Is Healing: Action Step

Tell your story to at least one new person today.

THE NEED TO
KNOW THAT I HAVE
BEEN HEARD

Let the wise listen and add to their learning.

(Proverbs 1:5)

When we know our words have been heard, we feel validated, supported, and cared for. There is a level of peace that comes from knowing that the people we are sharing our grief story and feelings with "get it." Once our words are heard regarding a particular or specific grief issue, we are free to move forward and tackle the next grief issue that we need to resolve.

When the words that we speak are not heard, we tend to get emotionally stuck for a while because we are experiencing more frustration and stress. Since the goal is moving forward and healing, the more extra stress that we can avoid, the better off we are.

If you are not able to speak the words of your story or are speaking the words but not being listened to, take a minute and find yourself on the following list.

Are you feeling?

☐ Frustrated   ☐ Vengeful

☐ Angry   ☐ Sad

☐ Fearful   ☐ Hopeless

☐ Depressed   ☐ Alone

It's easy for any or all of these feelings to manifest when we know that we have not been heard. These emotions also tend to get stirred up when people fail to understand that there are a lot of things we can't face or do right now. Here are a few common examples:

- Attending church the first few times after the death—but realizing after you sit down that you just can't stay—the grief is too overpowering. You leave.

- Finding that you are physically unable to get out of the car and go inside a certain building for an event that you got all dressed up for—because of memories related to your loved one and the building. You go back home.

- If your spouse has died, you may not be able to eat at home for a while—it's too lonely and painful. You eat out. Or the reverse. If you ate out all the time before the death, you may now find eating out painful and need to eat at home for a while.

- If your spouse has died, the need to continue to wear your wedding band when others feel you should remove it.

- If your spouse has died, you decide not to wear your wedding band anymore, and others think that you should still wear it.

If your family members and friends are not listening or are listening and telling you why you should not feel the way you do, etc., then it's time to either find a good support group or to make an appointment with your pastor, rabbi, priest, or a therapist who specializes in grief. You need to find someone who will listen to your words and hear what you are saying. There is a bonus that comes with sharing outside of our circle of family and friends. It's wonderful to have a place to go where it is safe and objective to share our complaints about our family members and friends who aren't listening. Every word of grief and frustration needs to be heard.

A Gem of Hope:

When you find yourself doubting your capacity to recover, be patient and realize that the grief process, though lengthy, ultimately does bring healing.

Grief Therapy, Karen Katafiasz [10]

The Destination Is
Healing: Action Step

Make a gratitude list. Even if you can only think of one thing to be grateful for, write it down.

_____

_____

_____

_____

_____

_____

_____

_____

_____

_____

_____

_____

_____

_____

_____

_____

_____

THE DANGER IN
STUFFING EMOTIONS

"What lies behind us and what lies before us are
tiny matters compared to what lies within us."

Ralph Waldo Emerson

When we don't speak the words of our grief, we end up
stuffing our emotions. Stuffing emotions is high risk
behavior that impacts us not only emotionally, but physically. However, there are situations and places where it is
sometimes necessary to refrain from speaking words of
sorrow and showing any emotion, even when we are ready
to explode with grief. Work and school are two of these
situations. Returning to work or school can be a diversion
and blessing for some people and a daily trial for others.
Many people are able to schedule in time for their emotional grief release and tears before or after work or school.
The rest of us wonder how they are able to manage this
feat.

The reality is there are times when it does not matter where we are or what the expectation of a particular
environment is—the grief explodes out of us. For example,
tears do not respect work place rules, nor follow them. This
is normal. However, every griever needs to understand that
trying to maintain a professional standard in a business,

school or similar environment is entirely different than stuffing emotional pain and never dealing with it. In his book *Deadly Emotions,* Dr. Don Colbert, M.D. shares:

> Repressing certain emotions can be healthy in the short term. And repressing an automatic response can give a person a little extra time in dealing with emotions that might completely overwhelm him if he experiences them all at once. This especially happens when a loved one dies. Have you ever noticed that the bereaved family sometimes seems to hold up better than others around them during the death of a loved one?
>
> What has happened is that their minds have repressed or blocked overwhelming grief responses for a short period. Grief stricken people may experience a state of denial for several days or even weeks until their emotions have a chance to catch up to the reality of their loss. This is a normal, healthy defensive action of the mind. What is not healthy is for a person to bury or deny unpleasant, overwhelming emotions indefinitely—emotions that would be far healthier for the person to confront and work through. When we pretend that all is well when all is not well, when we tell ourselves and others that nothing bad has happened when something very bad has happened, when we act as if we have suffered no loss or pain when we have suffered great loss or pain, it is then that we are stuffing what we should express. When a person begins to pack powerful and devastating emotions in the closet of his soul, he is setting himself up for trouble.[11]

While growing up you may have been asked, "What's wrong with you?" when you tried to express your emotions. Or, maybe you were told, "You shouldn't feel..." or "Boys (Big Girls) shouldn't cry." When we are taught or learn by example not to express emotions, we tend to automatically stuff negative feelings—many times without even realizing it. The problem is that denying emotions impacts healing in a negative way. Dr. Colbert goes on to explain that the result of not dealing with negative emotions is aches, pains and many times physical illness.

Renowned researcher Candace Pert, Ph.D., is the scientist who discovered the mind-body connection related to the role of neuropeptides, the chains of amino acids which are the communication link between the brain and the cells in the body. These information molecules, which she refers to as "molecules of emotion" actually carry a "photocopy" of each thought to every cell in our body. [12] What we think, feel *and* repress is continually transmitted and communicated throughout every body system and cell in the body, positive or negative! Dr. Pert shares this with us in her book, *Molecules of Emotion:*

> My research has shown me that when emotions are expressed—which is to say that the biochemicals that are the substrate of emotion are flowing freely—all systems are united and whole. When emotions are repressed, denied, not allowed to be whatever they may be, our network pathways get blocked, stopping the flow of vital feel-good, unifying chemicals that run both our biology and our behavior. This, I believe is the state of unhealed feeling we want so desperately to escape from. [13]

Since the importance of expressing and releasing emotions has been validated by research, we need to ask: Am I expressing the emotions that I am feeling in a constructive way? Or, am I stuffing negative emotions? Here are a few helpful ideas:

- First, you can share *all* your emotions with God, even your anger. He really can take it. Remember, we are made in his image. Incidentally, the Bible does not teach that it is a sin to experience emotions. It is how we choose to resolve our emotions, for example our anger, which can become an offense.

- Stand in front of a mirror and look directly into your own eyes. Speak the words of your pain aloud and let the tears flow. Some of us can only do this exercise when we are alone in the house.

- Each time that you are telling your story to "anyone" who will listen, add just a little bit of information that references how you are feeling. Sometimes when we deliberately add a brief explanation regarding how we feel—it becomes easier each time to share and express what we actually are feeling. Sharing is confidence building.

- Journal. Put the words of your feelings down on paper. Journaling is not an easy task for many people. Some of us are lucky if we can get more than a few sentences written in our journal at a time. On the contrary, we may know different people who write pages of words when they journal. We are all different, so don't let a friend who writes pages and pages intimidate you.

In addition, some people do not want anyone in this lifetime or the next to read the words in their personal journal. If this is you, you have options. For instance, write and then rip up the paper. The act of setting fire to the written word also works for some people, many of whom find this act empowering. If you decide to set fire to your writing, practice fire safety so that you don't burn your house down. An outside fire-pit works well.

- Pets are fabulous listeners, and a safe audience. Share your feelings with them.

- Grief support groups are full of people who share the experience of death. These people are willing to listen. Check with your local funeral home, hospice or community mental health agency to locate a grief support group in your area. Sometimes it is necessary to try a few different support groups out before you find one in which you feel comfortable. However, it's a good idea to give each group that you attend a chance. Go back at least three times before you make the decision to quit the group.

- Exercise is a stress reliever. Go to the gym or go for a walk. Remember, even walking to the mail box counts!

- The old adage, "you are what you eat," is true. Eating junk food depletes the body of the energy and strength that is needed in order to do the work of grief. Eat healthy and stay hydrated. Drink water.

A Gem of Hope:

It is possible to break the habit of stuffing emotions. Even if you can only express your feelings to the walls in your house or the flowers in your garden, it still counts!

The Destination Is Healing: Action Step

Try journaling. Express your words out loud on paper. Writing helps the brain to "re-wire."[14] The following are a few prompts to help you begin this process:

1. Today, I miss _____

2. My feelings are _____

3. I'll feel like I will go crazy if _____

_____

_____

_____

_____

_____

_____

_____

_____

_____

_____

TEARS CONTAIN
THE MIRACLE
OF HEALING

You number *and* record my wanderings; put my
tears into your bottle-are they not in your book?

(Psalms 56:8, AMP)

Did you know that beautifully designed glass bottles, often
found in Egyptian tombs, were used originally for burying
some of the mourners' tears with the body of the deceased?
Many of us wish that we could have put some of our tears
in a glass bottle and buried them with our loved one(s). It's
a shame that this symbolic and meaningful tradition was
abandoned long ago.

Today, we find that we live in a culture where we have
not only given up putting tears of grief in glass bottles, but
we are often times discouraged or told not to cry when
someone we love is in the process of dying or has died.
Unfortunately, for many people the value of tears has been
lost, but it's time for another shift in thinking—one that is
backed up by science. A good cry will make you feel better!

Because of studies done by Dr. William Frey, a bio-
chemist, and other scientists, we now know that the chemical composition of emotional tears is different than the

chemical composition of tears produced from, for instance, cutting up onions. Emotional tears contain levels of stress hormones, which means tears not only lubricate the eyes and membranes and bathe the eyes in lysozyme, the most effective antibacterial/antiviral agent known, but tears also serve as a release for stress toxins. These chemicals build up in the body when the body is under stress, and they are released or excreted in tears.

Adrenocorticotrophic hormone (ACTH) is one of the stress chemicals found in emotional tears. Concentrations of manganese (affects mood), leucine-enkephalin (helps control pain) and prolactin (hormone) are also found in emotional tears. As a result of these findings, the notion that tears do not serve any useful purpose is false. Crying is necessary for healing.

In fact, the latest research has shown that suppressing tears actually promotes more stress and increases the risk of some diseases.[15] The verdict is in, and it is scientific. Tears are normal and necessary for healing. God created us with emotions and he created the tears that belong to those emotions. Tears are not a sign of weakness, self pity or craziness. Tears are powerful agents of change and healing. Each emotional tear contains the miracle of healing.

So why do tears of grief trigger a negative response from some people? Based on our experience, we have concluded that tears of grief make a lot of people uncomfortable. The absence of tears makes it easier for people to pretend that all is "magically" well again. A negative response to tears by a friend, family member or co-worker doesn't have anything to do with you, the griever. It's about that particular someone projecting their own emotional uneasiness and trying to protect his or her own comfort zone. Tears of grief represent the fact that death can happen in anyone's family.

The clarity that death brings forces everyone involved to take a hard look at end of life realities and issues. For instance, dying for some is a slow and painful process, while others have no warning. In addition, their spouse could die next. Their child could die next. Their parent could die next. One of their siblings could die next. *They could die next.* Mortality becomes reality. Denial is easier in the absence of tears.

Maybe you were taught as a child not to cry. Maybe you were told that tears are a sign of weakness. If so, it's time to change your thinking. Give yourself permission to cry. Give your loved ones permission to cry. Let the tears flow and allow the miracle of healing to continue.

A Gem of Hope:

Crying is not about what other people think. Crying is about what you *know* you *need* to do in order to heal! Tears are a sign of great strength.

The Destination Is
Healing: Action Step

Just for fun, Google Dr. William Frey and tears. Information will come up on the incredible research done on tears by Dr. Frey and other scientists. Dr. Frey also wrote a book called *Crying: The Mystery of Tears*, Winston Press, Texas, 1977.

PITFALLS AND POTHOLES ALONG THE PATH

DEFINING A PITFALL AND A POTHOLE

I am rooted, established, strong, immovable, and determined.

(1 Peter 5:9, AMP)

According to *Webster's Collegiate Dictionary*: "A pitfall is a trap or a snare; specifically: a pit flimsily covered or camouflaged and used to capture and hold animals or men or a hidden not easily recognized danger or difficulty." A pothole is defined as a "pot shaped hole in the road surface."[16]

There are many experiences and emotionally camouflaged traps and snares along the path of grief that can land us in an emotional pothole. We addressed the first three in the previous two chapters. They are: failing to find words to define and express our loss, not speaking those words aloud, and not being heard. Neglecting to learn about the grief process and choosing not to do the work of grief will also land a griever in a pothole.

The grief process includes normal grief experiences that have pitfall and pothole potential. Unfortunately, these experiences are known for their ability to hold a griever emotionally hostage and for making the journey more difficult. Find yourself on the list below.

I am:

☐ FEELING OVERWHELMED.

☐ EXPERIENCING LACK OF SUPPORT.

☐ FRUSTRATED WITH THE WAY OTHERS RESPOND OR DON'T RESPOND.

☐ EXPERIENCING DISBELIEF BECAUSE FAMILY MEMBERS AND/OR FRIENDS ARE REFUSING TO TALK ABOUT THE DEATH.

☐ PART OF A GROUP OF MULTIPLE FAMILY MEMBERS LIVING UNDER ONE ROOF THAT ARE ALL GRIEVING DIFFERENTLY—AND GETTING ON EACH OTHER'S NERVES.

☐ STUFFING NEGATIVE EMOTIONS.

☐ TREATING MY PERSONAL GRIEF AS A "FORBIDDEN GRIEF" AND NOT SHARING

MY SORROW, DUE TO A PERCEIVED STIGMA
RELATED TO THE TYPE OF DEATH.

☐ TRYING TO ADJUST TO NEW RESPONSIBILITIES
AND ROLE CHANGES. (THE MORE ROLES AND
FUNCTIONS YOUR LOVED ONE, FILLED THE MORE
SECONDARY LOSS YOU WILL LIKELY FEEL. THE
SHORT LIST: BEST FRIEND, COMPANION, LOVER,
ACCOUNTANT, HANDYMAN, CO-PARENT, CHEF,
SOCIAL SECRETARY, TRAVEL COORDINATOR...)

☐ DEALING WITH IN-LAW PROBLEMS.

☐ DEALING WITH THE EMOTIONAL STRESS
OF LEARNING TO PARENT ALONE.

☐ DEALING WITH GRIEVING CHILDREN
THAT ARE ACTING OUT.

☐ MANAGING FINANCIAL PROBLEMS.

☐ FINDING WAYS TO AVOID OR NUMB MY
PAIN. (CONSTANTLY ON THE GO AND BUSY.
ALCOHOL OR DRUG ABUSE, ETC.)

☐ USING MY GRIEF TO MANIPULATE
FAMILY MEMBERS OR FRIENDS.

As we travel the path of grief, we learn the importance of resolving or avoiding emotional traps and snares. Here are a few basic pitfall and pothole strategies:

- Allow yourself to cry.

- Accept the fact that no two people grieve alike—that's okay!

- Talk about your loved one. Tell your story to every person that will listen.

- Find support.

- Get help for drug and/or alcohol abuse.

- Learn as much information about the grief process as possible.

- If you find that you are stuck in a pothole, choose to climb out. Based on the personal pothole experience of many, *there is always a way to climb out.* Sometimes we find that we need to climb out more than once. Acknowledging that we are stuck is the first step in the process. This is hard work.

- Ask God for help. At the same time be willing to do your part.

Grief is not usually perceived as "work." But the truth is, it is very hard work that requires a tremendous amount of emotional energy. It can be exhausting, so exhausting that even the smallest tasks seem huge. Grief is also overwhelming. You probably didn't expect that you would have to work so hard to get to a place of healing.

A Gem of Hope:

A pitfall or pothole can also be an opportunity for both personal growth and healing.

The Destination Is Healing: Action Step

"Either I will find a way, or I will make one."

Sir Philip Sidney

Make a list of things that you can begin doing or continue doing that will help you move forward.

_____

_____

_____

_____

_____

_____

_____

_____

_____

_____

_____

_____

_____

_____

LACK OF SUPPORT
TOPS THE
"PITFALL LIST"

He will not abandon me or leave me like an orphan
in the storm-he will come to me.

(John 14:18, TLB)

Lack of support is at the top of the "pitfall list" for many
grievers. Let's be honest, even when we are not dealing
with grief, we like to feel supported. When we receive
the support we need, we feel safe, comforted, valued and
sometimes even taken care of. Understandably, the desire
and need for support increases in the aftermath of the
death of someone that we love and cherish. Lack of support by family and friends during this period is frustrating
and aggravating.

The problem is unresolved disappointment from
unmet expectations can quickly spark negative feelings of
resentment, bitterness, and anger that are difficult to let
go of. Not getting the support that we need and expect
can become a huge pitfall with large pothole potential.
Relationships can easily become strained and sometimes
broken.

We frequently rely on family and friends to support us through a difficult time. And this is one of those times! Disappointment and anger start to brew when they don't, won't, or can't. Sometimes family members and friends are unable to assist because they live too far away. Other times, they live nearby, but they just aren't helpful. Occasionally, we realize that different family members or friends are going out of their way to avoid us. When this happens, it is confusing and hurtful. The reality is the majority of the time, friends and family members just have their own lives—which they seem to return to rather quickly. Let's take a look at some of the more commonly expressed needs and expectations. See if you can find yourself on the list below. What does being supported mean to you?

☐ DO I EXPECT TELEPHONE CALLS FROM MY FAMILY AND FRIENDS EVERY DAY?

☐ DO I EXPECT FAMILY AND FRIENDS TO STOP IN FOR A VISIT EVERY DAY?

☐ DO I EXPECT MY CHILDREN TO TAKE OVER DIFFERENT HOUSEHOLD CHORES? POSSIBLY DOING THE WASH? SHOPPING? CLEANING? MOWING THE LAWN?

☐ DO I EXPECT FAMILY OR FRIENDS TO DRIVE ME PLACES?

☐ DO I NEED SOMEONE TO PUMP THE GAS FOR MY CAR BECAUSE I DON'T KNOW HOW?

☐ DO I EXPECT TO BE TAKEN OUT TO
EAT AT LEAST ONCE A WEEK?

☐ DO I EXPECT COWORKERS TO CUT ME
SOME SLACK, GIVE ME SYMPATHY?

☐ DO I EXPECT MY PASTOR TO CALL DAILY
OR VISIT ON A WEEKLY BASIS?

☐ DOES SUPPORT MEAN KNOWING
SOMEONE IS PRAYING FOR ME DAILY?

☐ DO I HOPE FOR OR EXPECT FINANCIAL
ASSISTANCE FROM DIFFERENT
FAMILY MEMBERS OR FRIENDS?

☐ DO I EXPECT FAMILY AND FRIENDS TO
ASSIST ME WITH NEW DAYCARE NEEDS?

Question: Have you shared your needs and expectations with your family members and friends? Sometimes we assume that others automatically know what we need, when the fact is, they are often clueless. Communication is essential. Of course, it is very frustrating and irritating when we do share what we need and we still don't get a helpful response. When this happens, it's time for an expectation re-evaluation.

Sometimes, whether we want to admit it or not, we place unrealistic expectations on others. However, even if the expectation is realistic, if the "help" isn't going to happen, fair or not, it's time for a new plan. And this new plan starts with a major shift in thinking. This is what we want you to say out loud so that you can hear it in your own voice:

"I need to become my own number one supporter!"

We do hear what you are thinking... "Wait just a minute! I'm the one whose loved one has died! My family and friends should be doing the adapting and making the necessary changes needed to help me. I shouldn't have to change my expectations." We agree. Unfortunately, for most of us, it doesn't end up working out this way. And it's not fair, but the truth of the matter is the only person's thinking that any of us can change is our own.

We can't make other people do what they don't want to do, what they don't think they should have to do, what they don't have time to do, or be what they don't want to be. Part of this "I am my own number one supporter" plan usually means stepping out of our individual "comfort zone" and finding the support that we need from new sources. If your spouse or parent has died, it may be necessary to acquire a few new skills.

When we are overwhelmed with grief, it is difficult to think about learning something new. Quite frankly, learning a new skill can be unnerving and just plan scary. For instance, after the death of a loved one it is sometimes necessary to learn how to use the washing machine and dryer, the lawn mower or the stove, make lunches, car pool, pay bills, and possibly learn how to write a check...it's a never ending list. Role changes and new responsibilities are all part of creating a new life after the death of a loved one.

Many widows and widowers have to learn how to pump gas. The gas pump can be intimidating and scary the first few times you use it, but it can be mastered! It's powerful becoming your own number one supporter. Muster up your courage and don't underestimate your abilities. Many times, it helps to claim (Philippians 4:13):

"I can do everything through Him who gives me strength."

Sometimes the things that we think others ought to be doing for us are the things that we need to start learning to do for ourselves. Learning new skills is confidence building. Deciding to become your own best supporter is a huge step forward. Again, don't underestimate your abilities.

We know sometimes it may sound like we are overdoing pushing the importance of finding a support group, but truth be known, when family and friends let you down, a good support group is a blessing. The new friends you meet are all in the same type of situation. More often than not they are usually more than willing to share their skills. For instance, if you have never pumped gas or don't know how to use the washing machine, it's nice to have a friend who is willing show you how.

Learning, sharing, growing, and sometimes dragging each other along by the hand is what happens in a good group. If you're not ready for a group, please make an appointment to talk with your priest, rabbi, pastor, or find a good grief therapist. You need to find support!

A Gem of Hope:

"Attitude is a little thing that makes a big difference."

Winston Churchill

The Destination Is Healing: Action Step

Instead of thinking about annoying family and friends that aren't helpful and/or the new skills that you need to acquire, take a break. This is overwhelming. Take yourself out to a dinner and/or a movie. Maybe invite a special friend or family member to join you.

THE IMPORTANCE OF MONITORING YOUR THOUGHTS AS HEALING OCCURS

For as I think in my heart, so I am.

(Proverbs 23:7, AMP)

Early in grief, it is normal to experience a continuous cycle of thinking, feeling and re-living grief emotions and the physical pain, stress, and feelings that these emotions produce. This season of lamenting requires us to put words to our sorrow and cry out in grief. This season of thinking, feeling, re-living and lamenting *is necessary* for healing.

Many grievers (not all) experience a mental tape of the details and circumstances surrounding the death playing over and over again in their mind. This is a normal and common occurrence in the first months following the death. Continuously reviewing the details allows the griever to absorb what has happened a little bit at a time, which is necessary for healing.

Sometimes when we first notice that we're thinking about something other than this tape or other feelings related to the death, we feel like we are somehow forgetting about our loved one. This experience commonly produces a twinge of guilt which produces the confusing need to re-focus our thoughts immediately back to the tape and/or death memories and the conflicting desire to let go of the tape and/or death memories and move forward—*at the same time.*

Don't panic when this happens. Forgetting about your loved one is not what is happening. You will never forget about your loved one. Healing is what is occurring. This is the beginning of the normal process of filing special memories from your brain into the "retrievable" storage area in your heart, that special spot where memories are kept. It's time to make the choice to focus on new positive thoughts. This is hard grief work, which you can only start to do when you are ready to.

Sometimes we also feel guilty when we first experience our feelings settling down a bit. The level of emotional and physical stress produced by grief emotions momentarily diminishes on these occasions. Most of us enjoy these moments of brief relief because these moments allow us to feel "normal" again for a period of time. This isn't about forgetting either. This is the beginning of emotions attempting to feel comfortable together again (your emotions were comfortable together before the death) for *longer* periods of time. Each time emotions are able to settle back down together for a period of time, the duration or length of time they remain comfortable together tends to last longer. You are healing. Eventually, your emotions will be comfortable together again for the majority of the time.

It is also normal to get to a point when you tell yourself, "I don't want to think about the death constantly anymore." Some grievers seem to have an easier time moving their thinking along. Most of us really have to work at re-directing our thoughts to something positive and current. This, too, is an on-going process.

Normal grief thoughts and memories that we think, re-think, assimilate, but refuse to eventually let go of *have the potential to hold us emotionally hostage.* In the previous section, we discovered that what we think and feel is continuously transmitted throughout every body system and cell in our body. We begin to think the way we feel and feel the way we think. If it's important to understand how this cycle works under normal circumstances, it is critical when we are grieving. Because when we are grieving, it's easy for our thoughts and feelings to get stuck indefinitely in a negative cycle of thinking and feeling that can keep us stuck in our grief. In his book *Evolve your Brain*, Dr. Joe Dispenza, D.C., explains:

> Your every thought produces a biochemical reaction in the brain. The brain releases chemical signals that are transmitted to the body, where they act as messengers of thought. The thoughts produce the chemicals in the brain that allow your body to feel exactly the way that you were just thinking. So every thought produces a chemical that is matched by a feeling in your body.
>
> When the body responds to a thought by having a feeling, this initiates a response in the brain. The brain, which constantly monitors and evaluates the status of the body, notices that the body is feeling a certain way. In response to the

bodily feeling the brain generates thoughts that produce corresponding chemical messengers, you begin to *think* the way you are *feeling*. Thinking creates feeling, and then feeling creates thinking, in a continuous cycle.[17]

You need to find the words to express your grief, speak those words aloud, and know that you have been heard. You also need to pay attention to what you are thinking, feeling, and hanging on to. At some point, and you will intuitively know when this is, it will be time to begin the process of focusing your thinking on today and the future. Grief work is hard work.

A Gem of Hope:

When we understand the principle of the thinking-feeling loop, it's easier to mindfully direct our words and thoughts forward toward healing.

The Destination Is Healing: Action Step

Take a bookstore break. Head to your local bookstore, buy a coffee or hot chocolate, find a book or magazine, and locate a comfy chair.

COMPARING
EXPERIENCES
AND PAIN

I will restore health to you, and I will heal your
wounds, says the Lord.

(Jeremiah 30:17, AMP)

For some reason, during this season of struggling and just
trying to survive, it's not unusual to find ourselves compar-
ing our death experience and pain with others who are also
grieving and wondering whose pain is worse. The reality
is there is no way to compare pain and there is no reason
to, because for each of us, our own personal pain is worse.

Circumstances, "who" died, how many loved ones have
died, etc., all impact the grief experience. We each have
our own unique story and pain. What matters is that we
honor each other's pain and hold each other up as we heal.
We learn along the path of grief that for each individual,
the pain is not less or more than for anyone else—it just is.

Another common experience is trying to gauge our
own personal healing progress against how we *think* someone else is healing and progressing...or not healing and
progressing. Let it go.

A Gem of Hope:

"To thine own self be true."

William Shakespeare

The Destination Is Healing: Action Step

Write a goodbye letter to your loved one. Read your letter aloud. If you have children, encourage them to write a goodbye letter, too. If your children are younger, drawing a goodbye picture is helpful. A special family time where everyone reads his or her letter, or shares his or her picture, is a time of healing.

_____

_____

_____

_____

_____

_____

_____

_____

_____

_____

_____

THE BELONGINGS

SORTING, SAVING, AND PURGING OUR LOVED ONES' BELONGINGS... WITHOUT REGRET

God is my shield, my glory and the lifter of my head.

(Psalm 3:3, AMP)

There are people who sort, save, and purge in what appears to be a timely, orderly, and considerate fashion, making this task look easy—even though it rarely is. For most of us, just contemplating what to do with the belongings is so overwhelming that we lay our heads down and we don't want to lift them back up again. Working on this task frequently triggers physical and emotional exhaustion and feelings of dread, depression and anger. This is difficult grief work for most people.

Some individuals prefer to complete all or a portion of this task alone. For many of us, this is not an option because we have children who need and want to help. The potential for emotional combustion runs high when multiple grievers (multiple personalities, temperaments, expectations and multiple ways of dealing with personal grief) work on this task together. Even so, with information and a plan, it is possible to build relationships and heal while working on this task.

The good news is, unless some rare situation is making it necessary to deal with your loved one's belongings immediately, you don't need to do anything today, tomorrow, or even this month. If circumstances force you into a position where it is necessary to address your loved one's belongings before you are emotionally ready, find a trusted family member or friend to help you.

Many people have shared their personal "What-I-Did-with-the Belongings" success stories with us. Unfortunately, we have also heard many tragic stories. Families have been divided and relationships have been broken, all over the belongings. What we find ourselves doing or not doing with our loved one's belongings can land us, or another family member, smack in the middle of an emotional pitfall or pothole. Fortunately, "belonging" dynamics make sense and are easy to understand.

We sort though belongings and memories at the same time. Of course, some memories trigger sad feelings and tears. But other memories produce humor and laughter, which are also necessary for healing. A memory that makes one person laugh can make another person cry. Give yourself and others permission to cry and to laugh. It is very important to remember that no matter what happens to the belonging, we keep the memory.

The belongings are emotional connections and tangible links to the loved one who has died. We can see the belongings. We can touch the belongings. In some instances, we can still smell the scent of our deceased loved one on an item. It can be comforting to sit in his or her chair, sleep in his or her favorite shirt, or to lie down and cry in his or her bed. For many grievers, including children, touching, holding, sleeping in, wearing, having a personal keep-sake, and even smelling the deceased loved one on different items is a necessary component of healing. It's important to understand these needs.

Linda shares:

> Within days of Donald's death, I found myself bagging up his clothes and other items, in large black garbage bags. I fiercely dragged those bags down my driveway all the way to the curb. The act of bagging up Donald's clothes was empowering. Dragging the bags down to the curb and leaving them there for garbage pickup made me feel like I still had control over something. I was angry. I could hear the tape of my words playing over and over my head. "Quit smoking so you don't have a heart attack and die and leave me with two teenagers." I could not believe what I had begged him to stop doing had actually killed him!

Because I was acting out my anger, I didn't think to ask each of my children what they wanted to keep. I just started throwing things out. Fortunately, my children had the courage to call their grandpa and tell him what was going on. Grandpa arrived, sat me down, and very kindly explained to me that I needed to slow down and involve my children in the process. Ouch! For more than a few minutes, I was very angry at him, too. But in my heart, I knew he was right. Unfortunately, the garbage truck had already come and gone.

I apologized to each of my children for causing more grief and loss to deal with. For the next two years, as my teenage son worked through the most intense phase of his grief-related anger, he reminded me many times that I had thrown out items he wanted to keep. All I could do was keep apologizing. To alleviate my guilt, I remind myself that I was not in my "normal" state of mind at the time—I was grieving.

I learned the hard way that parenting grieving children is difficult and exhausting enough without the addition of avoidable new trauma and drama for everyone to deal with. Causing my children more grief and loss to deal with inadvertently produced more parenting grief work for me. After this incident, I made an effort to avoid making decisions that added to my parenting burden.

Occasionally, someone attends a New Hope group and admits that he or she piled up the belongings in their backyard and burned them. The majority of the time, this is not the best plan. Others choose to leave everything belonging to a loved one exactly where they were at the time of the death. One room or the entire house is turned into a shrine. Having a "shrine" for a time may be helpful, as long as you give yourself a time limit for keeping it. It's also not unusual to keep the door to a bedroom, den, or workshop closed with the intention of never opening it again. The problem is we know we need to address something behind the door. Give yourself a time limit on keeping the door closed.

A Gem of Hope:

Fortunately, for most of us, this task does not have to be completed in a day, a week, a month, or a year. You have time to come up with a workable, relationship-building, sorting, saving, and purging plan.

The Destination Is Healing: Action Step

Start small. Have you thrown out your loved one's toothbrush yet?

BELONGING BASICS

Be strong and courageous. Do not be terrified; do
not be discouraged, for the LORD your God will be
with you wherever you go.

(Joshua 1:9, AMP)

It's normal not to want to part with any of the belongings—ever. It is normal on one day to want to keep everything that belonged to your loved and then want to throw
it all out the next day. It is also normal to feel like you are
physically throwing out your loved one when you decide to
throw something out that belonged to him or her. Many
times the desire to cling to the belongings is intertwined
with the yearning and desire to somehow experience the
safety of the past again.

It is normal to wonder, "If I get rid of this, how will
I fill the space?" Empty space is something to be considered because you may not be ready to face an empty space.
Each individual's personal world gets redefined as spaces
are emptied and as sorting, saving, and purging occurs.
The decisions about what items to keep and re-organizing
these items within your household, is part of re-organizing
and creating a new life for yourself without your loved one.

When you decide to part with an item, you will find
healing in the ritual of saying goodbye to the item before

releasing it to someone else or to the garbage. Take your time, hold the object, say goodbye, let the tears fall. Each time you release an item, you accept the loss of your loved one just a bit more. Two different plans for sorting, saving, and purging are shared in section four of this chapter.

When multiple grievers work together on this emotionally charged and very personal task, each person is faced with a personal desire to do things his or her own way. This is not always possible. Since the desired result is healing and relationship building, not emotional combustion and fighting, communication and a plan are necessary. Boundaries and age appropriate, clear expectations need to be determined before you begin. You may need to be firm. You may need to be flexible. You may need to be really creative!

The decisions you make while sorting, saving, and purging will impact your relationships with all involved parties in either a positive or negative way. It's worth taking the time to consider two questions: Will my decision promote healing or will it sabotage healing? And will my decision promote a relationship, or will it sabotage a relationship?

Take a few minutes to clarify where you are. Find yourself on the list below.

☐   AM I READY? YOU WILL KNOW WHEN YOU
ARE READY. DO NOT LET FAMILY OR FRIENDS
PRESSURE YOU INTO BEGINNING THIS
TASK BEFORE YOU ARE READY. YOU WILL
KNOW WHEN YOU ARE PUTTING IT OFF.

☐ Do I need to take preventative action? You may find it necessary to make it clear to everyone that you do not want to come home and find that "they" have emptied your home of your loved one's possessions in an effort to "help" you. If this has already happened to you, without your consent, and you are angry, we are sorry. Try to keep in mind that the intention was to be helpful. The only thing that you can do now is work on forgiveness. Always remember, no matter what happens to a belonging, no one can take the memory away.

☐ I Need Comfort: It is normal, comforting, and healing to hold or hug clothing that belonged to your loved one. It is also normal to want to smell the scent of a loved one on his or her clothing. Sleeping in a shirt or pajamas that belonged to your loved one, holding his or her blanket, robe, etc. can be very consoling. It is not unusual for young children, teenagers or older children to find comfort wearing a sweater or shirt during the day and/or sleeping in clothing that belonged to a parent, grandparent or sibling.

☐ Everybody Wants Something! Don't let family or friends pressure you into giving away items that you're are not ready to

PART WITH. A KINDLY SPOKEN "NO" OR "I WILL
GET BACK TO YOU ON THAT" IS ACCEPTABLE.
NEVER FORGET THAT YOU ARE IN CHARGE.

☐ SET A DATE: SET A DATE TO START GOING
THROUGH THE BELONGINGS. IF THE DATE ARRIVES
AND YOU ARE NOT UP TO IT, BE FLEXIBLE WITH
YOURSELF AND POSTPONE IT UNTIL A BETTER DAY.

☐ STARTING AND STOPPING: MAKE SURE THAT
YOU, YOUR FAMILY MEMBERS, AND ANY FRIENDS
THAT ARE WORKING WITH YOU UNDERSTAND
THAT YOU (OR ONE OF THEM) MAY START THIS
PROCESS ONLY TO FIND THAT YOU JUST CAN'T
DO IT. IT'S OKAY TO PUT IT ASIDE FOR ANOTHER
DAY. THIS IS EXHAUSTING GRIEF WORK.

☐ YES, I AM SETTING CLEAR BOUNDARIES:
THERE IS NO SET TIME TABLE. FAMILY AND
FRIENDS MAY HAVE A DIFFERENT IDEA THAN
YOU DO ABOUT HOW MUCH HELP YOU ACTUALLY
WANT OR NEED FROM THEM. TALK OVER YOUR
EXPECTATIONS. THEY CAN'T READ YOUR MIND
AND YOU CAN'T READ ANYONE'S EITHER. HAVE
A PLAN AND A BACKUP PLAN BEFORE YOU START.
SOMETIMES, THERE ARE FAMILY SITUATIONS
THAT CALL FOR COMPLETING THIS TASK ALONE
WITHOUT THE HELP OF FAMILY OR FRIENDS.

☐ CONSULT AN EXPERT! BEFORE YOU SELL OR GIVE
ANYTHING AWAY OF VALUE, PROTECT YOUR OWN

INTEREST BY OBTAINING ADVICE AND APPRAISALS
FROM AT LEAST ONE EXPERT. WE DON'T ALWAYS
RECOGNIZE THE VALUE OF POSSESSIONS, SUCH
AS ART WORK, TOOLS, A TRACTOR, ETC. GETTING
ADVICE FROM AN EXPERT ELIMINATES YOU BEING
TAKEN ADVANTAGE OF. IF YOU ARE AWARE OF THE
VALUE OF ITEMS YOU CAN CHOOSE TO SELL OR GIVE
THE ITEMS AWAY WITHOUT ANY CONCERNS THAT
YOU MAY HAVE BEEN TAKEN ADVANTAGE OF. *A
WORD OF ADVICE FOR WOMEN*—MAKE YOURSELF
A TOOL BOX BEFORE YOU GIVE ANY TOOLS AWAY.

☐ FAMILY FIRST! ALLOW YOUR CHILDREN THE
OPPORTUNITY TO CHOOSE ITEMS THAT ARE
MEANINGFUL TO THEM. DON'T MAKE ASSUMPTIONS.
ASK. IF GIVING CHILDREN THE OPTION TO CHOOSE
WILL CAUSE A FAMILY WAR, YOU MAY FIND IT
NECESSARY TO DECIDE YOURSELF WHO GETS WHAT.

☐ I DON'T WANT TO PART WITH ANYTHING:
NOT WANTING TO PART WITH ANYTHING THAT
BELONGED TO YOUR LOVED ONE IS NORMAL AND
ACCEPTABLE. BUT EVENTUALLY YOU WILL HAVE
TO BEGIN THIS TASK. THE GOOD NEWS IS YOU
DON'T HAVE TO START THIS PROJECT TODAY.

☐ I FEEL LIKE I AM SNOOPING THROUGH MY
LOVED ONE'S PRIVATE PAPERS: IT IS NOT
UNUSUAL TO FEEL LIKE YOU ARE INVADING
YOUR LOVED ONE'S PRIVACY. FOR EXAMPLE,
THIS IS COMMON WHEN CLEANING OUT HIS

or her desk drawers or filing cabinet that is filled with personal records.

☐ I Can't Sleep In My Bed: A bed or bedroom set are belongings. It is not uncommon, especially after the death of a spouse, for the remaining spouse to have difficulty sleeping in the bed that he or she once shared. Many people eventually find that they need to invest in a new mattress or an entire new bedroom set in order to sleep. Sometimes re-decorating or changing rooms is helpful, too. You will need to figure out what works for you.

☐ Something New! Be creative. One woman made a vest out of her husband's ties. Someone else made a quilt out of her husband's ties. Another woman made teddy bears out of her son's flannel shirts.

☐ Helping Others! Unwanted clothing and other items can be given to organizations like the Salvation Army, Good Will or Purple Heart.

☐ Memories: Write your history. Organize pictures in books for different family members. You may want to take up scrapbooking.

◻ WHAT DO I DO WITH RESCUED MEMENTOS, PICTURES, CARDS AND OTHER TREASURES? A SPECIAL BOX OR CONTAINER IS WONDERFUL FOR HOLDING SPECIAL, MEANINGFUL MEMENTOS. WHENEVER YOU WANT YOU CAN TAKE OUT YOUR MEMORY BOX AND GO THROUGH THE ITEMS. A SPECIAL BOX FOR EACH FAMILY MEMBER IS ALSO A TERRIFIC IDEA.

Are you thinking that after you complete this task, you won't have anything to do? If so, one solution is to line up a few new projects to start once you complete this one. Sometimes it's helpful to have something to look forward to. It can also be helpful to fit in a new project while you are sorting, saving and purging. Be creative.

A Gem of Hope:

When you part with an item, you are only parting with the item, not the memory. You will always keep your memories tucked away in a special spot in your heart.

The Destination Is
Healing: Action Step

Consider different ways to involve any "grieving" children (no matter the age) in this task. Consider how each child is expressing his or her grief. Also, consider each child's age, personality, developmental stage, and any special needs.

_____

_____

_____

_____

_____

_____

_____

_____

_____

_____

_____

_____

_____

_____

_____

_____

_____

_____

_____

MEMENTOS AND LINKING ITEMS: IT'S ALL A MATTER OF PERCEPTION

Christ is seated in heavenly places and I am seated in him. He is above all principalities and powers and all things are under his feet.

(Ephesians 1:20–22, NKJV)

Many grief experts today divide the belongings of a deceased loved one into two categories: mementos or linking objects/items.[18] A memento is a personal possession that belonged to your loved one, which you decide to keep as a reminder. The emotional connection/attachment you have with the object is healthy and allows healing. A linking item, on the other hand, is a personal possession which triggers the opposite emotional response. The relationship with the item is not healthy or conducive for healing.

Examples of mementos are medals, a watch, pictures, trophies, uniforms, videos, a piano, ticket stubs, etc. These different items have significant meaning either for you or another family member or friend. Some people continue to display these items in their home or purchase/make a special box to keep them in. Occasionally, a memento won't fit in a house or in a box. For instance, one New Hope support group attendee kept a show car. There is no limit on the size of a memento.

A linking object is any object that links us to our deceased loved one with an unhealthy emotional connection. Believe it or not, these objects can hold us emotionally hostage and keep us stuck in our grief. The amazing thing is we sometimes don't even realize it! Keep in mind any object can be a linking item for someone and most importantly that every griever does not have a problem with objects turning into unhealthy linking items.

The standard list of linking objects, which is generally offered in most grief books, is a bit confusing. Typically the list includes the deceased's toothbrush, his or her shaving gear, aftershave, perfume, make-up, bottles of medication, etc. The problem is two of these items are mementos for many people. Over the years, we have had many grievers tell us that he or she has kept a bottle of perfume or aftershave—not as a linking item, but as a memento. These individuals find taking an occasional whiff comforting. We have never found a linking list that includes the most common offender either—the answering machine.

Many grievers eventually admit the answering machine, with the tape of his or her loved one's voice, held them hostage. Some people are unable to stop calling home and listening to the voice of their loved one. This obsession has been known to produce anger, depression and emotional turmoil—and children/teenagers are notorious for getting stuck in this negative cycle without the adults in their life realizing it. The voice mail on the cell phone of the deceased may present the same problem.

The reality is, calling home or calling the cell phone of the deceased and finding comfort in hearing his or her voice is normal for a period of time after a death. Many of us have done this. But at some point, and you will intuitively know when this is, it will be time to retire the recording. Many people keep the recording in their special memento box. Anytime you want to, you can pull it out and listen to it. Making the new recording is an opportunity for a family healing event, too. If your spouse has died and you want a male voice to answer your phone, have a male friend loan you his voice.

Again, it's necessary to understand that what is linking for one person is not for another person. Another example, which shows us just how different we all react, is one that involved Linda's son and his friend, who experienced the deaths of their fathers within a few months of each other.

Linda shares:

My son's friend was given his father's car to drive, and the result was positive. My son, on the other hand, started driving his father's truck, and the result was explosions of anger and depression. It took me a while to connect his behavior to time spent in the truck. Figuring out grieving children/ teenagers is exhausting.

One day while driving in the truck with him, I finally "got it." Our conversation that day revolved around memories of his father dying. My son witnessed his father slowly dying over a four hour period before I arrived at the hospital. He explained that these memories overtook him each time he drove the truck—and made him angry. While he was sharing, I started thinking back in time, recalling the many different incidences when his anger had spun out of control. I realized his combustible behavior was indeed related to spending time in the truck.

I knew the truck would have to go. But I would need a plan, because he didn't want to part with his father's truck. A *difficult* period of negotiation followed. Two weeks later, in agreement, we traded in the truck. This decision did cost a small sum of money, but I understood disconnecting my son from the truck was necessary for his healing. I did not want him stuck emotionally and not healing because of an unhealthy link to a truck. Coming up with money for a different vehicle was difficult, but cheaper than long term grief therapy.

Parenting grieving children and teenagers is complicated for the grieving parent(s) who is trying to figure out what the child needs for healing. Many times, the changes that need to be made or the therapy that is needed for a child to heal are financially expensive.

The "belonging" dynamics also impact extended family members and friends:

- The telephone stops ringing. Eventually, someone is honest and explains to you that everyone has grown weary of, or it is too traumatic for him or her to listen to a deceased person's voice answering the telephone.

- A friend finally admits that is too painful to visit your house now and see ____ empty chair.
- Friends stop visiting because the urn is on display.

The urn is a belonging that many of us don't consider.

Linda shares:

One of my friends would stand on the porch and visit because she just could not come in the house with "Donald" in it. I actually found this to be a bit amusing until I shared what was happening with my children. Both of my children took this opportunity to tell me that living with the urn "wigged" them out. A family meeting was held, and we decided it was time to bury Donald's ashes in the cemetery.

A Gem of Hope:

It is possible to creatively un-link yourself or a child from unhealthy connections to objects.

The Destination Is Healing: Action Step

Make a list of any objects that are keeping either you or one of your children stuck in grief. Start working on a healthy plan to disconnect.

_____

_____

_____

_____

_____

_____

_____

_____

_____

_____

_____

_____

_____

_____

_____

_____

_____

_____

"THE THREE-PILE PLAN" OR "THE DINING ROOM TABLE PLAN"

"Ambition is the fuel of achievement."

Joseph Epstein

The Three-Pile Plan

This plan has been handed down from one griever to the next because it works. It simplifies the process. Make three piles. The first pile is for items you want to keep. The second pile is for items you don't want to keep. The third pile is for items that you are unsure about. Put the items from the first pile away. Get rid of the items you do not want to keep. Box up and label items that you are unsure about and set them aside or store them in your basement. You can decide what to do with them later.

Most people do not complete this process in a day or even a week. And depending on how much you have to sort through, it could take a year or more. On some days it is just one drawer, one shelf, or one closet at a time. Other days, it is too painful to do anything—so we don't. It's okay to stop and start. It's okay to change your mind and retrieve items out of the garbage. When you are unsure, it is sometimes better just to leave the object where it is. You can decide later. This is especially true for large items. Be flexible with yourself and others who are helping you.

The Three-Pile Plan also works well when cleaning out a garage or a pole barn.

Linda shares:

> When Donald died, he left me with a pole barn full of his "treasures" and other people's "treasures," too. He was always bringing something home. He acquired his stash from stores, businesses, garage sales, and the widows from our church. These women knew who to call to pick up "treasures" that belonged to their beloved, deceased husbands. So when he died, I not only had his stuff to sort through, I had Mr. Millar's, Mr. McClung's...
>
> Donald's "treasures" made him a very happy man. And I am grateful that he enjoyed collecting them. But my happiness for him did not stop me, after a week of attempting to sort through tools, auto parts, and a lot of items that I did not know exactly what they were, from thinking, *It would be nice, in some instances, if husbands could take their "treasures" with them when they died.* I am certain I am not the first widow to think this thought!
>
> I decided it was time for a garage sale. Over the course of a few weeks, my son, my dad and I sorted, saved and discarded. My garage sale was advertised as a garage sale for men with a "free pile." Before the sun came up on the day of the sale, pick-up

trucks and vans were lined up and parked all the way down my street waiting!

I still chuckle when I recall this day and all the men filling up their vehicles with Donald's "treasures." Items from the "free pile" disappeared within a few hours. I am positive many wives were not chuckling when their husbands arrived home with the new "treasures." The bonus for me was I didn't have to pay for a dumpster!

The Dining Room Table Plan

"The Dining Room Table Plan" is another plan that works well. This plan came to Cathy's attention a few years back.

Cathy shares:

While visiting at the home of an older, widowed gentleman who had attended one of my support groups. I noticed that the top of his dining room table was covered with pairs of women's shoes. My curiosity got the best of me, so I asked him what he was doing. He explained to me that he was going through his wife's belongings and this particular day it was her shoes. Each week he went through different items. He also explained that he spent time with each item before he discarded it or boxed it up.

This plan worked for him, and it may work for you, too. Some people combine both plans. Figure out something that works for you.

Ultimately, if you really are stuck and need help moving forward in this area, professional help is an option. By professional, we mean either making an appointment with a grief therapist so you can figure out why you are stuck and what you can do about it, or hire professional movers/cleaners to help you. Again, it's a matter of figuring out what will work for you in your unique situation.

A Gem of Hope:

Some days, it is just one pair of shoes at a time or one drawer at a time. Some days, things just need to be left in the piles or on the table for another day.

The Destination Is Healing: Action Step

If you are up to it, clean out one drawer today.

IT'S NOT JUST
THE BELONGINGS:
EVERYTHING ELSE THAT
IS GOING ON IN YOUR
LIFE MATTERS

Thy word is a lamp unto my feet, and a light unto my path.

(Psalm 119:105, KJV)

Everything else that is going on in your life impacts how much time and energy you have for sorting, saving, purging and ultimately, healing. Even if the death of your loved one has left you without any sorting, saving and purging responsibilities, secondary loss, role changes and new responsibilities are overwhelmingly exhausting. What else is impacting *you*? Find yourself on the list below.

☐   NOW SOLE PARENT, JUGGLING WORK
     AND SMALL CHILDREN/TEENAGERS

☐   HAVE TO/ALREADY HAVE FOUND EMPLOYMENT/
     POSSIBLY WORKING MULTIPLE JOBS

☐   FINANCIAL PROBLEMS

☐ HAVE HEALTH ISSUES AND MY LOVED ONE
WAS MY MAIN SOURCE OF SUPPORT

☐ ALL/MOST HOUSEHOLD CHORES
ARE NOW MY RESPONSIBILITY

☐ MUST LEARN HOW TO DRIVE

☐ MUST LEARN HOW TO PAY BILLS

☐ NOW RESPONSIBLE FOR
AUTOMOBILE MAINTENANCE

☐ EACH FAMILY MEMBER HAS A DIFFERENT
OPINION REGARDING WHAT I SHOULD DO OR
WHAT I NEED TO DO—WHICH IS CONFUSING

☐ I HAVE GRIEVING CHILDREN/TEENAGERS/
YOUNG ADULTS THAT I AM RESPONSIBLE FOR

☐ THE DEATH WAS A SUICIDE WHICH HAS
COMPLICATED MY GRIEF AND THE GRIEF
OF EACH PERSON IN MY FAMILY

☐ I AM EXHAUSTED FROM CARE-GIVING DURING THE
ILLNESS AND DEATH PROCESS OF MY LOVED ONE

☐ I LOST MY CARE-GIVING JOB (EVEN THOUGH THIS
RESPONSIBILITY WAS CARRIED OUT IN LOVE, CARE-
GIVING RESPONSIBILITIES ALSO FUNCTION AS A

job—a 24/7 job many times) when my loved
one died. Now what do I do with my time?

☐ My loved one is gone—there is
no one else to consider

☐ I have to move

It's a wonder anything gets done at all. Sometimes we are
just too tired and overwhelmed to sort, save, and purge.
Other times, there are more important issues that need
to be addressed, particularly financial issues and paper-
work. Grieving children are also exhausting to parent.
Older adult children many times are more exhausting to
deal with than younger children. Grievers grieving differently can strain relationships, particularly the marriage
relationship. For instance, one person wants pictures of the
deceased displayed and the other wants them put away.
Working though and accepting each other's grieving dif-
ferences is also exhausting.

Grieving secondary losses adds to the fatigue. For
example: if you were your loved one's caregiver, you have
lost your "job." You did it out of love, but it was work.
Experiencing the loss of the daily routine and responsibilities which you are accustomed to is overwhelming and can
also be exhausting, sometimes more exhausting than being
a caregiver 24/7. It takes a while to adjust to all the changes
and different or new responsibilities or lack of responsibilities. But, there are things you can do that will help.

While this process of adapting to change is going on, it's important to make time for new activities. Before you lay your head down on your pillow to go to sleep each night, you need to have a plan for the next day. Even if you don't end up doing it, have a plan and a back-up plan. Give yourself something to look forward to. Give your children something to look forward to. In between all the changes and sorting, saving and purging, everyone, including you, has to learn how to have fun again.

Activity possibilities:

- Make a weekly trip to the library. Explore new subjects and new authors. Take your children along, and make it a family event. Most libraries have special events for children.

- Check your local newspaper for daily events and activities that are open to the public. Take your children.

- Attend a play at your local high school. Make it a family event.

- Learn about investing/estate planning. Classes are offered through continuing education. Or attend free seminars for the purpose of learning—not necessarily making a commitment.

- Check out your local YMCA. Most have a pool and offer classes for all ages.

- Visit your local book store. Take your children.

- Make an appointment to have lunch/dinner with a friend each week.

- Join a book club.

- Volunteer at your local school.

- If you're married and grieving the death of one or more children, it's important to make the choice to stay connected with your spouse. Pray together. Go on a date once a week. Talk, cry. Turn to each other—not away from each other. Decide to walk down the path of grief together and to end up at the destination of healing, acceptance and new beginnings together. Don't allow grief to throw you into two different potholes!

Warning

- If you are widowed, you may be finding that you are enjoying spending more time with your grandchildren. Be aware this usually is not the best time to commit to becoming the full-time, long-term babysitter *just so that you have something to do*. It is very possible (based on the experience of many) that within just a few months of making this huge commitment, you will be asking yourself, *What was I thinking?*

- Volunteering at the hospital/hospice is an option. Just remember that you are grieving and vulnerable. Being around illness and death may be too hard to handle right now.

- Continuing your education may be necessary. Keep in mind that concentrating is difficult during this time. Retention and recall abilities are affected by grief.

A Gem of Hope:

It is possible for everyone in your family to once again embrace new goals and activities.

The Destination Is Healing: Action Step

It's time for a new daily habit. Before you lay your head down on your pillow tonight, come up with a plan for tomorrow that includes one new activity.

_____

_____

_____

_____

_____

_____

_____

_____

_____

_____

_____

ANGER

BUT...I'M NOT ANGRY

"Anger is like a red light flashing on the car's dash.
It indicates that something needs attention."

Gary Chapman, *Anger, Handling a Powerful
Emotion In a Healthy Way.*[19]

Let's begin with a few questions. Can you find yourself on
the list below?

☐   Do I find myself getting upset
over things that seem minor and
I wonder why I am so upset?

☐   Do I take my anger out on the people I
really care about and who care about me?

☐   Is there something concerning
the circumstances of my loved
one's death that angers me?

☐   AM I FEELING EXTRA SENSITIVE, IRRITABLE AND FRUSTRATED?

☐   COULD I BE ANGRY AND NOT EVEN KNOW IT?

Sometimes we tell ourselves, "I'm not angry."

Linda shares:

I remember telling different people, "I'm not angry." I also remember the day my physician challenged those words. I had presented to his office, multiple times, with one virus after the other. He had the "nerve" (my first thought) to tell me what I needed to do in order to get well. He said I should address my death-related anger. I was stunned.

I looked directly into his eyes and confidently said, "But—I am not angry." He looked directly back into my eyes, sweetly chuckled, turned around and walked out of the exam room. He never looked back as he grabbed the door handle and gently closed the door. I sat in reflective silence for about five minutes before I realized he was not coming back—and I hated to admit it, but I also knew he was correct.

For the first time I was able to admit to myself that I had been working very hard at avoiding my anger. Over the years I had fallen into a habit of never addressing my feelings of anger when I experienced them. I also realized I didn't know how. I slowly got up and left the room, only to find my physician waiting at the end of the hallway for me. He looked at me and smiled and said, "You can do this, too." In that moment I realized that I indeed could—even though I didn't want to. I was exhausted from all the grief work I was already doing; I couldn't believe there was more personal grief work for me to do.

This encounter with my doctor didn't happen immediately after Donald died, either. It happened over two years after his death. This incident also occurred after I had been co-facilitating New Hope support groups for a few months. Thank goodness my physician understood the role unresolved anger plays in healing and confronted me.

Anger is sneaky sometimes because it impacts us in degrees. Most of us don't realize that the feelings associated with the emotion of anger can range from feelings of minor irritation and frustration to intense rage. If you don't yell and scream, you may not realize you're angry. On the other hand, if you happen to be a yeller and a screamer and your anger voice has been strangely silenced by grief, feelings of anger may be hard to recognize right now.

Anger is easier to recognize when we understand that the emotion itself is neither good nor bad. Anger, many times, is the flashing red light at an intersection in life that warns us that we need to stop, look, listen and resolve issues. Furthermore, it's important not to confuse feelings of anger with the actions that we take while we are angry. It's the actions that we take that can become an offense.

One action that many of us commonly take is to ignore or stuff our anger. This gets us into trouble both physically and emotionally. As we already mentioned in chapter three, stuffing emotions has consequences. Many times, we fail to realize we are holding unto unresolved anger until we find ourselves physically sick or stuck in an emotional "anger pothole."

Over the years, we have found anger to be the emotion most prevalent in grieving people. Feelings of hurt, frustration, confusion, rejection, and fear commonly result in anger. Helplessness or feelings of loss of control over life can also trigger angry feelings. The truth is, after the death of a loved one, all these feelings automatically show up for most of us. We don't even have to go looking for them!

WORDS THAT DESCRIBE ANGER:

- Annoyance
- Irritability
- Irritation
- Frustration
- Passion
- Resentment
- Fury

- Exasperation
- Temper
- Antagonism
- Wrath
- Rage
- Bitterness

The word "anger" is derived from the Latin word *angere,* which means, "to strangle." True to its meaning, anger has the potential to emotionally and physically strangle (choke, smother or suffocate) us. In addition, unresolved anger is the number one cause of unfinished, complicated grieving. In other words, you won't be able to get to a place of positive healing if you are stuck in the stranglehold of unresolved anger.

Under normal life circumstances, angry feelings many times occur when our plans and goals are interrupted. Death is the ultimate plan and goal interrupter. Death has stolen your loved one and robbed not only your loved one of his or her plans and goals, but you of plans and goals as well. It is normal after a death to be angry at different people and things. You have a lot to be angry about!

Common anger recipients:

- Unfairness of the world: "Why did it happen to her? She was such a good person." "He was too young."

- Doctors and paramedics: Maybe it was a misdiagnosis or late diagnoses. Maybe the paramedics didn't arrive as quickly as you thought they should have. Maybe he or she wasn't as sensitive as you thought they should have been.

- Friends: You may feel as though your friends have not been available when you have needed them. Sometimes it seems like friends immediately return back to their lives and forget about us. Other times we can't believe what friends say to us. Or maybe you have a friend who is a "boundary buster" and is making an attempt to run your life by insisting on making decisions for you now—with good intentions, of course.

- The person responsible for your loved one's death: The drunk driver. The reckless driver. The murderer. The terrorist. Or the person who was unintentionally responsible.

- The person who died: If he/she hadn't smoked. If he or she took their life and left you with the complicated grief of suicide to deal with. Or perhaps it's the fact you now have to deal with legal work and/or learn how to manage finances. Maybe it's a change of lifestyle because there was no insurance money—or the insurance money went to the children from the first marriage. Or maybe you are angry just because your loved one has left you all alone in this world!

- You: Sometimes we think we should have done this or that and we get angry at ourselves because we didn't. Other times we wish we hadn't done something. Maybe you were the one driving the car or that left the pool gate open. Your intention was not to harm, and professional help may be necessary in order for you to sort everything out. Get it. Don't allow yourself to get stuck in this "pothole."

Figuring out anger signals and responses is a difficult process for most of us under normal conditions. After a death the lens we view life though is colored by the raw pain of grief. This adds to the confusion and time it takes to sort out feelings. Fortunately, even when we are grieving it is possible to separate and sort out different feelings and address them. It is possible to learn to recognize anger signals and choose to resolve anger in constructive ways.

You are a special and unique individual. Anger may not be the first issue or feeling which you personally need to address. It can be helpful to visualize different emotions and feelings as layers on an onion. We peel back each layer of emotion slowly and heal. Some feelings have more than one layer of emotion which needs to be addressed and peeled off for healing. And each of us peels off and works through emotional layers and feelings in our own unique order and time.

A Gem of Hope:

Almost everyone gets angry at some point after the death of a loved one. This is because the person who died was a very important part of your life.

The Destination Is Healing: Action Step

Read the opening list of questions again. If you have not done so already, answer each question with honesty.

IDENTIFYING THE
STRANGLEHOLD
OF ANGER

"About 20 percent of the general population have levels of hostility that are high enough to be dangerous to their health—that's one in five!" [20]

Deadly Emotions, Dr. Don Colbert, M.D.

Unresolved anger has been linked to physical pain, heart rate changes, blood pressure changes, lung function issues, and changes in digestive track activity. [21] This is why it is so important for each of us to figure out how we are directing our personal anger. Many experts in the field of anger resolution frequently refer to the following three ways that people direct their anger. Can you identify with any of the following?

☐ ANGER DIRECTED AT SELF: MANY PEOPLE DIRECT THEIR ANGER INWARD (STUFF) AND DON'T EVEN REALIZE IT. WHEN WE DO THIS OUR ANGER SITS IN THE CORE OF OUR BEING AND BURNS AND FESTERS. AFTER SIZZLING FOR A WHILE, THIS ANGER SUDDENLY EXPLODES OUTWARD IN ANGRY OUTBURSTS THAT ARE DIRECTED AT UNDESERVING AND UNSUSPECTING PEOPLE. SOME ANGER EXPERTS REFER TO THIS EXPLOSION OF ANGER AS "FREE FLOATING ANGER." ANYTHING CAN SET IT OFF AND THE ANGER MAY SEEM IRRATIONAL.

Cathy shares:

After Don died, I had to go to the hardware store and buy a new part for the toilet. Once in the store, it took me a while to find the part I needed, but I did. Navigating the hardware store was a new and exhausting adventure. By the time I got in line to pay, I had had it. As the clerk was ringing me up, he began explaining to me what my "husband" needed to know about replacing the part. Before he could finish, I exploded. I explained I didn't have a husband—because he was dead. I also let him know that I was going to install the part myself. I paid and stomped out of the store. I am sure, even today, nearly three decades later, this man still remembers me.

☐ ANGER DIRECTED AT OTHERS: THIS TYPE OF ANGER IS DIRECTED OUTWARD. THIS TYPE OF

ANGER BUILDS ON ITSELF, CAN LEAD TO RAGE AND IS ALSO TYPICALLY DIRECTED OR DISPLACED ONTO THE WRONG PERSON, AT THE WRONG PLACE, AND AT THE WRONG TIME.

AN EXAMPLE OF THIS WOULD BE A TEENAGE GIRL WHO BECOMES REBELLIOUS, DISRESPECTFUL AND TAKES HER ANGER AND RAGE ABOUT HER BROTHER'S DEATH OUT ON HER PARENTS. ANOTHER EXAMPLE IS A PERSONAL ONE.

Linda shares:

My son directed most of his anger and rage at me after the death of his father. At one point, he got in my face and yelled, "I wish it had been you who died and not dad!" Those words pierced my heart. All I know is God took over and I couldn't speak. In that moment, I realized I could not take his words personally and make his outburst about me, or we would both be in trouble. The reality was that I was the safe person for my son to share his angry feelings with. He needed to be heard and he needed help—professional help. Parenting grieving children is exhausting.

Constructive or Motivational Anger: Anger that is used as a positive motivator. It causes us to take action and remove obstacles so we can reach our goals. It is more quickly released and prompts us to respond in a positive manner. An example of constructive anger:

MADD (Mothers Against Drunk Drivers) was founded by Candy Lightner after her thirteen-year-old daughter was killed by a drunk driver. Her grief was turned into intense anger when a California judge gave the drunk driver—a repeated offender—a light sentence. Anger provoked by injustice motivated her to establish the national organization MADD.

God created us in his image. God created the emotion of anger. In his book *Anger, Handling a Powerful Emotion In a Healthy Way*, author Gary Chapman shares:

> Anger is not evil; anger is not sinful; anger is not a part of our fallen nature; anger is not Satan at work in our lives. Quite the contrary. Anger is evidence that we are made in God's image; it demonstrates that we still have some concern for justice and righteousness in spite of our fallen estate. The capacity for anger is strong evidence that we are more than mere animals. It reveals our concern for rightness, justice, and fairness. The experience of anger is evidence of our nobility, not our depravity.
>
> We should thank God for our capacity to experience anger. When one ceases to experience anger, one has lost her sense of moral concern. Without moral concern, the world would be a dreadful place indeed. He goes on to state: "But I believe that *human anger is designed by God to motivate us to take constructive action* in the face of wrongdoing or when facing injustice.[22]

A Gem of Hope:

When a loved one dies, we face the injustice and the unfairness of death. There is a lot to be angry about. However, it is possible to use our anger to move forward in the healing process. Grief work is hard work.

The Destination Is Healing: Action Step

Identify the different ways that you are directing your anger. Identify who you are directing your anger at.

_____

_____

_____

_____

_____

_____

_____

_____

_____

_____

_____

_____

_____

THE 4 A'S OF ANGER:

To everything there is a season, and a time for every
matter or purpose under heaven.

(Ecclesiastes 3:1, AMP)

Edgar Jackson shares an excellent four-point strategy for
anger resolution in his book *The Many Faces of Grief.*

THE 4 A's OF ANGER BY EDGAR JACKSON:

1. Admit it. Perhaps the hardest thing to do with anger
   is to admit that that is what it really is. We have been
   trained to cover up our anger so completely that we
   ourselves are fooled by the many varied devices we
   use to hide it. But when there is a great amount of
   emotion directed outward or inward, it usually implies
   anger, and we might as well face it.

2. Analyze it. Once we have admitted our anger, we
   must lift it up to objective examination. Ask yourself,
   "Why am I so upset? Does my attitude or behavior
   make sense?" Back off and look at the anger to see if
   you can find out where the large burst of emotion for
   the small cause really came from. Has someone sat in
   your favorite chair or parked in your parking space?

Has someone said something that stepped on your favorite prejudice or threatened your chance to make a little extra money? Has someone said something that came close to exposing some feeling that you wanted to keep hidden? Such questions open the way for an evaluation of your emotion.

3. Act on it. The third step (having realized where the anger comes from) is to seek a wise and healthful way of working it out of your system. Do not suppress it further, for it will surely surface again. Rather, do something with it that will not hurt you or anyone else. Take a long walk, chop wood, play golf, or read a detective story. But know what you are doing and why—to get the full benefit from the acting out.

4. Abandon it. Fourth, make sure you believe that your anger is not worth what it costs in inner stress or fractured human relations. Anger can be a weak spot in your personality. It can complicate and destroy life. It isn't worth the price, so it should be abandoned for insight, understanding and healthful action. [23]

One widow shared that her anger release was making homemade bread. For her, the act of kneading the dough released anger. When she was done kneading and releasing her anger, she baked delicious loaves of bread which she shared with family and friends. Here are some other ideas for acting on and abandoning anger:

• If you are angry with the deceased, go to the cemetery and talk to him or her. Talk to a picture of your loved.

Or you can set up two chairs. You sit in one and visualize your loved one or the offender sitting directly in front of you in the other chair. Share your feelings of anger with them.

- Walking, jogging, swimming, and biking are all excellent stress and anger releasers.

- Write a letter to your loved one or to the person/ people you are angry with. Express your feelings by using "I" statements. If you decide to write a letter to an offender, don't mail it out. Set it aside for at least a month. Review again and decide if it is appropriate to send.

- Invest in a punching bag. This works well for many people. But sometimes children/teenagers get more worked up and angry while punching the bag. Retire the bag if the result is over stimulation.

- Journal. Write about all the aspects of your anger.

A Gem of Hope:

It is possible to release and act on anger in a positive way. Include your children. Start walking, running, biking or baking bread together. Invest in journals for everyone. Write!

The Destination Is
Healing: Action Step

This action step is also from *The Many Faces of Grief* by Edgar Jackson.

> When grief triggers the reservoir of anger that life has stored up, it is well to recognize it for what it is and to work it through in creative and civilized ways...Anger is a part of life. The question is whether it will be used to become more destructive of self and others, or whether it can lead to creative insight and useful action. [24]

Choose creative insight and useful action!

ANGER AT GOD

Surely God is my help; the LORD is the one who
sustains me.

(Psalm 54:4)

If you are not angry with God, or if you don't believe in
God, you will still find the information covered in this section useful. This information is helpful because the death
of your loved one has most likely left at least one of your
family members or friends angry at God. Understanding
this type of anger will allow you to support others who are
dealing with this issue.

It is not unusual to experience feeling angry with God
after the death of a close loved one. For some of us, this is
one of the toughest angers to deal with. If you had a strong
faith in God before the death, and your faith was a daily
source of comfort and support, you may be dealing with a
major secondary loss if you can't get comfort from God as
you have in the past.

Anger with God doesn't have anything to do with how
"deep" or "strong" someone's faith is. The anger that we
feel when someone that we love dies is really anger related
to what we believe God didn't do—because we believe he
could have or he should have spared our loved one. We
also find ourselves asking God, "Why?" And do you know

what? You have the right to ask why. Some people may try to tell you that you don't, but you do. It's normal to want an explanation! We want life to make sense again. So we ask him:

- God, why did you allow this murder to happen? You could have stopped it.

- God, why didn't you answer my prayers for healing? You are God. You have the power to heal.

- God, why didn't you stop the accident from happening? You could have!

Asking why is not a sign of weakness or irreverence. It is simply a normal part of the grief process and sorting out anger. Unfortunately, what we slowly discover is that God doesn't give us an answer to the "Why" question very often. This adds to our frustration many times. Even Billy Graham, when interviewed, didn't have an answer to the "Why" question after 9/11.

For many of us, death shakes the foundation we have built our faith on. This leads to more questions:

- Do I really believe that God is in control and that he knows the beginning from the end?

- How can I trust God again?

- Do I need to forgive God?

- Did God really do anything wrong?

- Why do I need to deal with my anger toward God?

Anger toward God, if prolonged, shuts us off from God, and this is a time that we need his love and grace more than ever. Bitterness will only make suffering worse. It is helpful when we remember that we are created in God's image. In Genesis 1:27 we read,

God created man in his own image...

God created us in his image—with emotions and specifically the emotion of anger. Anger is part of our humanity. So what does God expect us to do with our anger?

In Ephesians 4:26 we read,

In your anger do not sin: Do not let the sun go down while you are still angry, and do not give the devil a foothold.

Notice this verse says, "In your anger do not sin." It doesn't say feeling angry is a sin. It is what we do with our anger that can become an offence.

After a death, many times, it is not possible to resolve angry feelings before the sun sets. Understanding the principle of letting go is what matters. Many times we find that we need to continually work at resolving anger because the stranglehold is so severe. When resolution takes more than one sunset, God understands. He knows you are sincerely working on anger resolution. Furthermore, since we are created in his image, he is also not surprised by our anger and frustration with him. He understands it. He can take it.

Unfortunately, another problem for many of us is that we either were incorrectly taught, or wrongly assumed, that it is a sin to experience or express anger. Consequently, admitting anger is admitting sinning. Admitting we are angry with God not only seems extra sinful, but very wrong. Then a death happens! We don't know what to do with the death-related anger we are experiencing. What is even more overwhelming is we don't know what to do with the anger we feel toward God. It you believe feeling the emotion of anger is a sin then it's time for a shift in your thinking based on biblical truth. Feeling anger and verbally expressing our feelings, even to God, is not a sin.

Many times after a death, forgiving God is how we reestablish our relationship with God. Cathy shares:

> After spending some time being angry about my circumstances and asking, "Why" over and over again, I made a conscious choice to forgive God and to stop asking why this happened. I told him "I trust you and I forgive you." It was only then that I was able to let go of the anger and move on in a healthy way.

Do you need to forgive God?

Do you need to decide to trust God again?

Trust in the LORD with all your heart and lean not on your own understanding; in all your ways acknowledge him, and he will make your paths straight. Do not be wise in your own eyes; fear the LORD and shun evil. This will bring health to your body and nourishment to your bones.

(Proverbs 3:5–7)

A Gem of Hope:

God never stops loving us, no matter how loud we yell and scream at him. He even loves us when we find that we can't even pray.

The Destination Is Healing: Action Step

Even if you don't want to anymore, and even if you don't end up staying for the whole service, this is not the time to stop attending church. Spiritual healing is also a part of grief work. Trust God for a new vision for your future.

FORGIVENESS

"Forgiving gets its unique beauty from the healing
it brings to the saddest of all the pains."

Forgive & Forget, Lewis B. Smedes [25]

Forgiveness is a choice. Many times it is a difficult choice.

Linda shares:

> I have found myself, on more than one occasion,
> stubbornly refusing to forgive and wishing there
> was some way to "zap" the offender with a small
> bolt of lightning...of course, just enough to inflict
> pain. My desire to "zap" the offender flows out of
> the negative feelings that I am experiencing at the
> time. These feelings are wrapped around my fierce
> desire to punish the offender. I want the offender
> to admit responsibility and to hurt as badly as I do.
> I want justice.

Be honest, if "zapping" doesn't cross your mind, what does?
How do you want to punish the offender? How badly do
you want the offender to hurt?

Have you also noticed when the offender isn't aware,
for whatever reason, that he or she has committed an

offense, or if the offender doesn't believe he or she is responsible—or just doesn't care—it's the person who refuses to forgive who experiences the anger surge and who suffers from additional physical and emotional stress? Not the offender! Sometimes we also find ourselves standing back and watching as the offender strolls happily along on his or her merry way through life, seemingly unaffected. And many times, even if punishment was handed down, for instance by a court of law, we still are not satisfied.

The truth each of us ultimately must come to understand about unforgiveness and spiteful, revengeful thinking is that *unfortunately* it doesn't punish the offender. It only "zaps" us emotionally and physically when we refuse to forgive. In addition, the poisonous venom produced by unforgiving spills over and contaminates other important relationships, including the relationship we have with ourselves.

Over the years, many of us have had the unfortunate experience of having an encounter with a bitter, snarly person who is difficult to be around. Many times, he or she is consumed with an offense which occurred twenty years ago...and he or she is still talking about the offense as if it happened yesterday. The intention was probably not to become the bitter, unforgiving person who is stuck in the past—the one that no one wants to be around—but this can very easily happen to any of us. Life is too short. Relationships with family and friends are too important. This is why it's important to forgive.

In chapter three, we learned how critical it is for each of us to pay attention to what we think about, feel, and what we emotionally decide to hang on to. This awareness is necessary because what we think and feel seems to have an automatic tendency to turn into a continuous cycle of thinking the way we feel and feeling the way we think, either negative or positive. After a death it's easy to get trapped in an unproductive, unhealthy, negative thinking and emotionally feeling cycle that keeps us from forgiving. If you are unwilling or unable to forgive, you are most likely stuck in the "pothole" of unforgiveness.

You are not alone. Getting stuck in the "pothole" of unforgiveness is common after a death. What does forgiving mean and why we need to forgive? Let's begin with what it means to forgive.

WHEN I FORGIVE I:

- Absolve
- Acquit
- Exonerate
- Impart Mercy
- Pardon

In order to absolve, acquit, exonerate, show mercy or to pardon someone, it is necessary *to choose* to let go of the bitterness, frustration, hate, resentment, and other toxic emotions that we are feeling toward that person. Forgiveness is not about what someone deserves. Forgiveness is not about who is right and who is wrong. In fact, when we choose to forgive someone it does not mean what was done wasn't wrong, doesn't matter, doesn't hurt, or that justice should not be served. Forgiving also does not mean we will or should forget what was done.

Forgiving involves separating the act from the offending person and letting go of all the negative emotions involved. Sometimes, in order to achieve forgiveness, we have to make the decision to accept what now is and intentionally decide to let go of what should or could have been. Forgiving also means choosing to let go of the desire to seek justice and punishment. When we forgive we release ourselves from all the pain that comes from unforgiveness: anger, hate, the desire for revenge, etc. We need to choose to forgive until we experience the unique peace that only the complete relinquishing of unforgiveness produces. Forgiveness is a process. Forgiveness is hard grief work.

Is there someone you need to forgive?

- Doctors or paramedics?
- A friend?
- A family member?
- The person responsible for your loved one's death?
- The person who died?
- You?
- God?

Do you need to forgive yourself for a healthy outcome? Maybe you were the one driving the car when the accident occurred, or maybe you were the one who left the gate to the pool open, or maybe you didn't realize your spouse was actually having a heart attack—whatever the human error, real or imagined, forgiving yourself is necessary for your own healing.

Jesus died for our sins and mistakes. Ask God to forgive you and then *accept* his forgiveness the first time you ask. Receive his mercy, grace and love. Allow yourself to move forward toward the destination of healing, acceptance and new beginnings. If you feel your action or inaction somehow contributed to the death, you need to remind yourself that your intention was not to cause harm. And, do you know what? God already knows this and he doesn't want you stuck in the "pothole" of unforgiveness. He has a plan and purpose for your life!

If in your case the offender's intention was harm and death for your loved one, God knows this, too. Release the offender to God for punishment. Trust him to take care of it. God doesn't want *you* stuck in the "pothole" of unforgiveness forever either. He has a plan and purpose for your life, too!

Once again, we want you to visualize a large onion with many layers. As each of us begins the painful process of forgiving ourselves or others, we slowly begin the painful process of peeling back and removing each and every layer of bitterness, resentment, frustration, hate and *regret* that we are clinging to. In his book, *Deadly Emotions,* Dr. Don Colbert, M.D. shares:

Forgiveness releases layers of hurt and heals the raw, jagged edges of emotional pain. Saying "I forgive" is like taking an emotional shower. Forgiveness cleanses and frees the entrapped soul.[26]

Forgiveness is for the person doing the forgiving. Choosing to forgive frees the person doing the forgiving. The choice to forgive will allow you to take a huge step forward along the path of grief toward the destination of healing, acceptance and new beginnings. Here are a few helpful forgiveness strategies:

- Journal. Let the tears flow. Write the words of your pain. Include why you don't want to forgive. Include why *you need* to forgive. For every negative feeling you write down, write down a positive feeling. Set short and long term forgiving goals. Be specific. Write down where you want to be on your journey of forgiveness a month from now, six months from now and a year from now.

- Write a letter to the offender detailing how you feel. *Don't mail it or give it to him or her.* Set aside *for a least* a month. You may decide not to send it.

- Sit down in a chair and put another chair in front of you. Imagine the offender sitting in the chair. Communicate your pain—and your words of forgiveness. Let the tears flow.

- If applicable, write yourself a letter of forgiveness.

- Exercise: walk, run, bike, hike, golf, dance...movement is healing.

- You are what you eat. Eat healthy and hydrate with water.

- At least once a day look directly into a mirror and make eye contact with yourself. Speak these words aloud: "I am able, willing and ready to forgive_____. I release myself from feelings of unforgiveness (name the feelings you are experiencing aloud) because I want to move forward and heal." If you need to forgive yourself speak these words aloud: "I am able, willing and ready and I choose to forgive myself. I am worthy of forgiveness and healing."

- Get your Bible out and read every verse on forgiveness. The verses are listed in the back of the Bible in the concordance.

A Gem of Hope:

Blessed are they whose transgressions are forgiven, whose sins (*and mistakes*) are covered. Blessed is the man whose sin (*and mistakes*) the LORD will never count against him.

(Romans 4:7–8, italics added by authors)

The Destination Is
Healing: Action Step

Make the choice today to free yourself from the bondage of unforgiveness and choose to forgive. If you find that you are unable to forgive and to let go of the bitterness, frustration, anger and resentment that you are feeling... professional help may be beneficial.

DEALING WITH FEELINGS

GUILT

"Nothing is more wretched than the mind of a man conscious of guilt."

Plautus

After the death of a close loved one, it is not unusual to experience feelings of self condemnation, blame, regret and remorse and guilt. Let's begin by reviewing a few common grief related guilt triggers. Can you identify with anything on the list below?

COMMON GUILT TRIGGERS:

☐ I RECEIVED AN INHERITANCE.

☐ I RECEIVED LIFE INSURANCE MONEY.

☐ I WAS NOT THERE WHEN MY LOVED ONE DIED.

☐ I SURVIVED. MY LOVED ONE DID NOT.

☐ I PROMISED MY DYING LOVED ONE THAT I WOULD TAKE CARE OF CERTAIN FAMILY MEMBERS. I DON'T WANT TO DO THIS. I CAN'T DO THIS.

☐ I REGRET THE HARSH WORDS THAT I SPOKE TO MY LOVED ONE BEFORE HE OR SHE DIED.

☐ I REGRET THAT ALL WE DID WAS FIGHT.

☐ I REGRET NOT TELLING MY LOVED ONE I LOVED HIM/HER.

☐ I REGRET THAT I WAS NOT SPEAKING TO MY LOVED ONE AT THE TIME OF HIS OR HER DEATH.

☐ DUE TO RELATIONSHIP ISSUES, I REALLY DON'T MISS MY LOVED ONE.

☐ I AM ENJOYING GOING PLACES AND DOING THINGS WITHOUT MY LOVED ONE.

☐ I LAUGHED AGAIN. MY SENSE OF HUMOR IS RETURNING.

☐ I REGRET NOT HAVING THE CHANCE TO SAY GOODBYE.

☐ OTHER: _____.

Let's take a closer look at a few of these. Receiving an inheritance or life insurance money was your loved one's way of taking care of you. Unfortunately, upon receipt of these items or funds, some grievers quickly spend or give away all the money or the items because he or she doesn't feel they deserve them. Many times guilt is also experienced because of how the money or items were acquired. Again, providing for you was your loved one's way of taking care of you.

Decide not to act on the impulse to get rid of things or to give away money or to go on an excessive spending spree, because you will probably regret doing so later. Instead, hire a CPA and financial planner. One educational option is to attend a Dave Ramsey Financial University Freedom series at a local church. (For information: www. daveramsey.com) Even if you don't think so right now, you may need this money to live off of some day. Don't let family or friends "guilt" you into giving them things or money, either.

Maybe your relationship with the deceased was difficult and you are not missing him or her. You are not the first griever to be consumed with feelings of relief and not feelings of sadness. If your relationship with the deceased was complicated and difficult, you may find that you need professional help in order to move forward.

Writing a goodbye letter is helpful if you didn't have the opportunity to say goodbye. Sometimes going to the cemetery and saying goodbye is helpful, too. If you are regretting harsh words that you spoke or not telling your loved one that you loved him or her, write a letter of apology. If you're feeling guilty because you are enjoying going places without your loved one, decide today to give yourself permission to just enjoy it.

Learning the basics about guilt can also be helpful. Many grief therapists divide guilt into two different categories. Let's take a look at them.

1. Appropriate (rational) guilt: this is guilt due to something we've done wrong, that we know we've done or something that we may have done on purpose. For instance:

   • "I knew the car needed new tires."

   • "I should not have let him/her drive drunk."

2. Inappropriate (irrational) guilt: this is guilt due to something we may have done that we did not do intentionally or as a way to hurt ourselves or others. Regret can also be a form of inappropriate guilt. It's often something we didn't do that we wished we had done. This is the "If only" or "I should have" guilt.
   "If only I had spent more time..."
   "If only I had responded sooner."
   "If only I had told her that I loved her more."
   "I should have retired when he wanted me to."
   "I should have known that she was sick."

Most of the time the regret that we feel is based on unrealistic expectations that we have set for ourselves regarding what we can and can't control, and what we think that we should, would, or could have done about something related to the death. Adding to the overwhelming emotional burden is that in times of crisis we have the tendency to focus on the negative.

Allow yourself time to process and to sort out any guilt feelings that you are experiencing. It is important to recognize that appropriate guilt, inappropriate guilt, and regret, all have the capability of holding someone emotionally hostage. Self condemnation will only keep you stuck where you are at. Sometimes, as we discussed in the previous chapter, forgiveness of self is necessary for healing. If you find that you are stuck in a "pothole" of guilt and regret...and unforgiveness of self, decide immediatley not to stay there. Accept God's forgiveness. God's plan and purpose for your life is not for you to live your life stuck in a "pothole" of guilt and regret. Get professional help if you need to.

A Gem of Hope:

Most relationships have a certain amount of ambivalence—good and bad. After a death it's normal to experience some regret and wish we'd done some things differently.

The Destination Is Healing: Action Step

It's healing to laugh again. It is healing to have fun again. When you have a few moments of fun or hear yourself laughing, make the choice to let go of any irrational and normal grief guilt that you are feeling and embrace the moment. Your loved one would want you to be happy and to have fun again. Laughter is healing.

NORMAL GRIEF
DEPRESSION

"Because acute grief often produces depressive reactions, it is important for the bereaved person to understand what is happening within him."

Edgar Jackson, *The Many Faces of Grief*[7]

Depression is impacted by stress, lack of sleep and poor nutrition. After a death we experience the highest stress level possible, we often can't sleep and we tend to forget about healthy eating. These normal grief reactions contribute to normal grief depression. It's difficult to look beyond discouragement and the past and believe in new beginnings. It's even harder to let go of disappointment and believe for a better tomorrow, and it's really easy and normal to be consumed by despair and loss of hope. Fortunately, with information, normal grief depression is manageable.

The first step in dealing with grief depression is to realize that a certain amount of depression during your bereavement time is normal and to be expected. Your life has changed drastically and loneliness, the additional responsibilities, and thoughts related to an unknown and a very different future can lead to feelings of depression. Grief depression produces many physical and emotional responses that are normal for grief and these are usually temporary. Let's take a look at some normal grief responses.

Do you find that activities that you used to enjoy are not enjoyable anymore? Do you find your energy level depleted? How about your motivation to do things you feel you should do or used to want to do. Is that motivation gone? Are there certain times of the day when you tend to get in a slump or feel depressed? A lot of people feel depressed upon waking in the morning. If morning is a time when depression hits you and a symptom of this difficulty is getting out of bed, you need to do something about it.

Many young widows and widowers have no choice about getting up in the morning. They have children who need attention or an employer who is expecting them. If you don't have a job, children or pets that need your attention, you need to find a reason to get up in the morning. What about an exercise class or an arrangement with a neighbor to meet each morning for a walk? We have a tendency to follow through on our commitments and to not want to disappoint someone who is expecting us. What about taking on a volunteer commitment that requires you to be somewhere in the morning? If someone is relying on you, you'll probably want to follow through.

Another reason that people often feel depressed is because they feel that their purpose for living is gone. This is a little different for the younger widowed person, since often there are children to be considered. If you feel that your life is meaningless and this causes you to feel depressed, allow yourself to have a "mini-pity party." Set a limit on how long you'll allow yourself to feel this way, and then begin to focus on the positive things about you that may temporarily be hidden.

For example, what personal strengths will you be able to draw on as you move through your grief? Are you a natural leader, good listener, do you practice hospitality, or even in more practical terms, are you good at fixing things? Make a list of your strengths, and then determine how each of these strengths can be used to help yourself and, in time, help others. The Destination Is Healing: Action Step in this section will help you to explore this area.

There are also things that you can do to combat depression:

- Do something physical. Walk, run, bicycle, swim, yoga...

- Adopt a pet.

- Have a plan for each day, night and weekend.

- Eat healthy food and hydrate with water.

- Get together with friends.

- If you can't sleep at night, fit in naps.

- Keep up with your body maintenance. Shave, keep hair trimmed, and wear make-up...

- Get a massage. Touch is healing.

- If you have children, involve them in a "family combat depression plan." Make sure they are eating healthy and hydrating with water, exercising, hanging out with friends, etc. Get them involved in planning events. Remember too, your children, who are also grieving, need you to be emotionally and physically healthy. They have already lost a loved one to death. Don't allow depression to steal you from them. You are needed. And part of God's plan and purpose for your life involves you being a part of your family and friends' lives.

Sometimes we become concerned and wonder if what we are experiencing is actually normal grief depression or if it is clinical depression. The following information from the American Cancer Society will help you to distinguish between the two.

> Distinguishing between grief and clinical depression isn't always easy, since they share many symptoms. However, there are always ways to tell the difference. Remember grief is like a roller coaster. It involves a wide variety of emotions and a mix of good and bad days. Even when you're in the middle of the grieving process, you will have moments of pleasure and happiness. With depression, on the other hand, the feelings of emptiness and despair are constant.
> Other symptoms that suggest depression, not just grief:
>
> • Intense, pervasive sense of guilt.
>
> • Thoughts of suicide or a preoccupation with dying.
>
> • Feelings of hopelessness or worthlessness.

- Slow speech or body movements
- Inability to function at work, home, and/or school
- Seeing or hearing things that aren't there [28]

If you unsure about what type of depression you are experiencing, or if you aren't sure if you need more help, make an appointment with a grief professional and find out. Most people who are grieving find that they do not need to seek out professional help or take anti-depressants in order to deal with normal grief depression. However, many of us don't fall in the "most people" category and this is okay. If you need professional help, find it. If medication is needed, take it. Monitor your medication along with your doctor for the desired result. You need to be able to function while on the medication in order to do the work of grief.

Unfortunately, you may encounter people who believe that depression is only linked to sin in someone's life. Not confessing or repenting of sin may cause depression at times, but sin is not the cause of all depression. People who have a relationship with God are just as prone to depression as those who don't. Sin is not the cause of normal grief depression, death is.

A Gem of Hope:

Normal grief depression is normal after the death of a close loved one.

The Destination Is
Healing: Action Step

Complete the "Finding Me Again" section on the next page.

Complete the Following:

The best depression buster is taking the focus off of self and reaching out to help others. In order to do this you need to find yourself again. Strengths, gifts and talents get hidden under grief. This exercise is designed to help you find yourself again and set some new goals.

Check off the personal characteristics below that apply to you.

Fill in the Finding Me Again chart on the next page. Be creative when deciding how you can use your strengths. Do you want to volunteer? Tutor children? Help out at your local school? Have a tea party? Have a card party? Find a part time job? Teach a class?

Do not dwell on your liabilities. But do come up with a few ideas for dealing with them.

Write down three short-term goals and three long-term goals. Dream a little. Is there something you have wanted to do or somewhere you have always wanted to travel?

- [ ] Active
- [ ] Adventurous
- [ ] Achiever
- [ ] Athletic
- [ ] Attractive
- [ ] Ambitious
- [ ] Articulate
- [ ] Artistic
- [ ] Balanced
- [ ] Bright
- [ ] Cheerful
- [ ] Culinary Artist
- [ ] Compassionate
- [ ] Conservative
- [ ] Creative
- [ ] Curious

- [ ] Cynical
- [ ] Dependable
- [ ] Easy-Going
- [ ] Effervescent
- [ ] Elegant
- [ ] Energetic
- [ ] Enthusiastic
- [ ] Exciting
- [ ] Expressive
- [ ] Extroverted
- [ ] Flexible
- [ ] Frank
- [ ] Fun-Loving
- [ ] Generous
- [ ] Gentle
- [ ] Gracious

- [ ] HAVE INTEGRITY
- [ ] HONEST
- [ ] IMPULSIVE
- [ ] INDEPENDENT
- [ ] INSPIRING
- [ ] INTELLIGENT
- [ ] INVENTIVE
- [ ] JOVIAL
- [ ] LAID BACK
- [ ] LISTENER
- [ ] NONCONFORMIST
- [ ] NON JUDGMENTAL
- [ ] OPEN-MINDED
- [ ] OPTIMISTIC
- [ ] OUTGOING
- [ ] PATIENT
- [ ] PERSISTENT
- [ ] PERSONABLE
- [ ] POSITIVE OUTLOOK
- [ ] POSITIVE THINKER
- [ ] QUIET
- [ ] SECURE
- [ ] SELF-ASSURED
- [ ] SELF-RELIANT
- [ ] SENSE OF HUMOR
- [ ] SENSITIVE
- [ ] SHY
- [ ] SINCERE
- [ ] SPIRITUAL
- [ ] SPONTANEOUS
- [ ] STABLE

☐ Strong	☐ Versatile
☐ Successful	☐ Vulnerable
☐ Supportive	☐ Warm
☐ Tender	☐ Witty
☐ Thoughtful	☐ Wise
☐ Understanding	☐ Young-at-Heart
☐ Unselfish	☐ Zany

Finding Me Again

LIST STRENGTHS AND ASSETS

1. _____

2. _____

3. _____

4. _____

How can my strengths/assets be used to benefit me and/or others?

_____

_____

_____

_____

_____

_____

List Only 1 Weakness/Liability

1. _____

What Can I do about this?

_____

_____

_____

_____

List 3 Short Term Goals

1. _____
2. _____
3. _____

List 3 Long Term Goals

1. _____
2. _____
3. _____

CHANGES IN
FRIENDSHIPS

"Nothing but heaven itself is better than a friend who is really a friend."

Plautus

Some individuals don't experience any negative relational issues after a death. However, many of us have found ourselves examining different friendship and possibly family relationships and wondering, "Who are these people?" Do you feel as if you don't have anything in common with one or possibly all of your friends now that your loved one is dead? Are you hurt because someone that you really thought was a close, dependable friend is now avoiding you? Are you wondering if you will ever fit in socially anywhere again? If your spouse has died are you feeling like a "third wheel" now? Are these normal responses? Yes!

Typically, we meet people where we live, go to school, work, shop, workout, volunteer, vacation and where we attend church. Some of our relationships start early in life and continue into old age. We also have relationships with people that we have come to know through our deceased loved one and his or her activities: work, school, vacations, growing up, etc., and possibly the local motorcycle club. Over the years many of these people become more than acquaintances. Our primary relationships are comfortable, familiar, and we understand the history of each relationship and how we fit into each relationship.

Usually, we don't give much thought to how comfortable (or uncomfortable) we are in our personal friendship situations, until a death changes the relationship dynamics by removing someone permanently. Sometimes that "someone" is the glue who held different friendships together. When the cord of friendship is severed by death, the rhythm, balance and authenticity of each relationship within the remaining group of friends is challenged. Everyone involved has to grieve. At the same time, as mentioned in chapter one, everyone involved has a brain and heart now involved in the process of adjusting and "re-wiring"[29] to an environment which no longer includes the deceased.

Many times friends work through their own grief issues and continue to move forward along the path of grief with us, supporting us, all the way to the destination of healing, acceptance and new beginnings. The outcome is positive. Unfortunately, other times, the internal relationship stressors and changes produced by the death cause the comfort level within the friendship to drop, sometimes drastically. The outcome many times is that we remain friends, but not close friends. Or sadly, sometimes the end result is the death of the friendship. The death of a friendship is a hurtful secondary loss which also needs to be grieved.

Let's explore a few more common normal responses and the "why" factor:

- Response: You are noticing that different people are avoiding you. Or someone will engage you in conversation, but he/she will not talk about the deceased.

- Why: Death has become a reality. It could happen to him/her next! Give people time to adjust. You can decide later if the friendship is worth a continued investment on your part.

- Response: Your deceased child's friends stop coming over.

- Why: Your child's friends are also grieving. Many times people don't know what to say or how to act. Sharing memories, hugs, and tears is healing. Invite them to celebrate your deceased child's life by engaging them in a memorial service. Support healing.

- Response: Since the death of your spouse, a few of your same sex friends have stopped calling you.

- Why: You are a reminder that his or her spouse could die next! And, as unbelievable as this next explanation is, it's unfortunately true and common. You are now a threat to your friend's marriage! Many times he/she is thinking that you will steal their spouse! Yes, before you have even had enough time to realize that you are now actually single once again, concern about spouse stealing has already begun. Our suggestion is to find the humor in this type of situation and move on.

- Response: You are older and one of your parents has died. A friend has shared with you that he or she expects you should be "over it" quickly.

- Why: Each person has been reminded that his or her parent could die next. Another observation that we have made is that for some reason, when people don't live with their parents anymore and one or both die, friends and sometimes family members wrongly believe the grieving process is easier because the parties involved were no longer living under the same roof. Hopefully, these friends and/or family members will eventually gain a better understanding of the grief process.

- Response: Your sibling or parent has died and several of your friends won't talk about it.

- Why: This may be the first experience that anyone you know has had with death. Each person is now faced with the reality that one of his or her siblings or parents could die next. Many times fear takes over. Not knowing what to say or even if it's okay to bring up the subject of the deceased can keep someone from sharing. Sometimes it is necessary to give someone permission to talk about the death and related issues. Sharing that you want and need to talk about the deceased is the first step.

- Response: Your spouse has died and you no longer feel like you belong in your couple friendships.

- Why: The dynamics within each couple friendship have changed. You are now single and creating a new life as a single. Your friends are still married and have each other. The death of your spouse has only changed *your* entire life. Sometimes, even when we stay connected with our couple friends, we sometimes feel like we don't have much in common with them anymore. It is normal and healthy to seek out friends who share and understand this new experience firsthand. But, it is wise to stay in touch with everyone who loves you.

Even friendships that you maintained separately from your loved one may be feeling uncomfortable right now. Many times, this turmoil has nothing to do with anyone else and everything to do with us and the conflicting emotions of grief we are experiencing. The changes brought by death are overwhelming. You probably have never had to function under so much stress! Give yourself a chance to get your own personal rhythm and balance back. Give others a chance to do the same.

A Gem of Hope:

As the rhythm and balance returns in your life, the rhythm and balance in your "true" friendships will also return. Healing is a process that takes time.

The Destination Is Healing: Action Step

Don't let the "pitfall" experience of loneliness while you're trying to figure out your friendships land you in a "pothole." Instead, take action. Look over the following list. Check off ideas that will work for you and pick out one to do today.

Ideas to Combat Loneliness

- ☐ GET ORGANIZED. ORGANIZE YOUR HOUSEHOLD FILES, YOUR RECIPE FILES, OR ANY OTHER FILES THAT YOU HAVE.

- ☐ WRITE IN YOUR JOURNAL.

- ☐ CLEAN A CLOSET.

- ☐ GET OUT IN THE YARD AND DIG. SPLURGE ON SOME BEAUTIFUL FLOWERS. BEAUTY IS UPLIFTING.

- ☐ GO TO A MOVIE. IF IT'S SOMETHING THAT YOU ENJOY, YOU'LL GET LOST IN IT AND NOT THINK ABOUT YOUR LONELINESS.

- ☐ CALL SOMEONE ELSE WHO MAY BE LONELY AND BE LONELY TOGETHER. A FUNNY THING WILL HAPPEN AND YOU WON'T BE LONELY ANYMORE.

- ☐ PUT YOUR OLD PHOTOS TOGETHER IN A SCRAPBOOK. CRY AS YOU FACE THE MEMORIES AND HEAL. YOU'LL FIND THAT YOU'LL FEEL BETTER AFTER YOU'RE FINISHED.

- ☐ TAKE A COURSE. EXERCISE YOUR MIND.

- ☐ TAKE UP A NEW SPORT OR GO BACK TO AN OLD ONE. WALK, JOG, TAKE TENNIS LESSONS,

OR GO FOR A SWIM OR RIDE A BIKE. EXERCISE
IS ONE OF THE BEST CURES FOR STRESS.

- ☐ TRY A NEW RECIPE AND INVITE
  SOMEONE OVER TO TRY IT.

- ☐ PAINT A ROOM OR A PICTURE.

- ☐ REDECORATE.

- ☐ GO THROUGH YOUR CLOSET AND WEED OUT
  WHAT YOU HAVEN'T WORN IN A YEAR. MAKE A
  LIST OF WHAT YOU NEED. GO SHOPPING AND PICK
  UP A FEW OF THE NEEDED CLOTHING ITEMS.

- ☐ TAKE A TRIP. IF YOU HAD FRIENDS THAT INVITED
  YOU TO COME FOR A VISIT, TAKE THEM UP ON
  IT. YOU NEEDN'T STAY LONG. BUT VISIT WITH
  FRIENDS WHO ARE UPLIFTING AND SUPPORTIVE.

- ☐ PLAN SOMETHING DIFFERENT THAT
  YOU HAVE ALWAYS WANTED TO DO.

- ☐ GET A HAIRCUT.

- ☐ PURCHASE NEW MAKE-UP. A
  MAKEOVER IS UPLIFTING.

- ☐ JOIN THE YMCA. THE CLASSES ARE
  GEARED FOR ALL AGES AND STAGES.

- ☐ CLEAN YOUR HOUSE.

WORDS WITH FANGS:
OH, THE THINGS
PEOPLE SAY

And he shook the beast into the fire, and felt no harm.

(Acts 28:5, KJV)

In the Bible in Acts 28, we learn about one of the Apostle Paul's many adventures. This particular time he was marooned on the island of Malta. Paul and other crew members collected sticks of wood for a fire they were trying to keep going. When Paul laid his bundle down into the fire, a viper that was hiding in the sticks charged out and sunk its fangs into his hand, injecting poison. He shook his hand violently, until the snake released his fangs and fell back into the fire. For hours the island natives watched and waited for Paul to die. He didn't. So they decided he was God.

One can only imagine the interesting conversations Paul had with different people on the island as he explained that he was not God, but that everyone had, in fact, witnessed a "God" miracle. This story is actually also symbolic of the words that we often hear after the death of a loved one.

Most people speak caring and encouraging words to us after a death. Unfortunately, there are times when the words that are spoken to us have "fangs" that latch into us with a poisonous emotional grip! And, when we don't realize that we need to "shake the words off," we can get in trouble because words have pitfall and pothole potential.

The following is the "I Can't Believe What I Am Hearing" shortlist. Can you personally identify with any of these?

☐ "I UNDERSTAND HOW YOU FEEL." (NO YOU DON'T!)

☐ "TIME WILL HEAL." (IT HURTS NOW AND TIME IS NOT WHAT HEALS!)

☐ "YOU'RE TOO YOUNG TO BE A WIDOW/ WIDOWER." (NO KIDDING!)

☐ "YOU'RE YOUNG AND YOU CAN GET MARRIED AGAIN." (I CAN'T EVEN IMAGINE THAT RIGHT NOW!)

☐ "CALL ME FOR LUNCH DURING THE WEEK." (I'M LONELY AT NIGHT AND ON THE WEEKENDS!)

☐ "CALL ME AND WE CAN GET TOGETHER." (I AM FEELING SO VULNERABLE, WHAT IF YOU REJECT ME WHEN I CALL?)

☐ "YOU'RE SO LUCKY YOU HAVE CHILDREN." (I AM OVERWHELMED WITH MY PARENTING

RESPONSIBILITIES. I AM ALSO WORRIED THAT DEATH IS GOING TO STEAL MY CHILDREN NOW!)

☐ "YOU ARE SO LUCKY THAT YOU HAVE OTHER CHILDREN." (MY OTHER CHILDREN DON'T MAKE ME MISS MY CHILD WHO DIED ANY LESS!)

☐ "YOU CAN HAVE ANOTHER BABY." (I DON'T WANT ANOTHER BABY! I WANT MY BABY BACK!)

☐ "YOU'RE LUCKY YOU DON'T HAVE CHILDREN." (BIG OUCH!)

☐ "YOU'RE VERY FORTUNATE THAT YOUR CHILDREN ARE GROWN AND ON THEIR OWN." (I STILL HAVE TO WATCH MY CHILDREN GRIEVE AND STRUGGLE! AND, IF THEY STILL LIVED AT HOME I WOULD NOT BE SO LONELY!)

☐ "AT LEAST YOU HAD THIRTY YEARS WITH YOUR SPOUSE. YOU SHOULD BE GRATEFUL." (WHO SAID I WASN'T GRATEFUL! I AM LONELY!)

☐ "YOU WERE ONLY MARRIED A FEW YEARS, (OR ENGAGED) SO IT WILL BE EASIER TO GET OVER." (YOU HAVE GOT TO BE KIDDING ME!)

☐ "HOW MUCH LIFE INSURANCE MONEY DID YOU GET?" (NONE OF YOUR BUSINESS!)

☐ "You must be rich now." (No, I am broke. But it's really none of your business. The money went to the children from the first marriage.)

☐ "Could I borrow some money?" (No! I am not the bank or a vulnerable target. Find someone else to be your "cash cow.")

☐ "You are so lucky because you get to do what you want now." (I have always done what I wanted!)

☐ "You are so lucky because you get to do what you want now." (I am and I am feeling guilty about it!)

☐ "How about going out dancing Friday night?" (You have got to be kidding me. My spouse's body is not even cold yet and you are married!)

☐ "God does not give us more than we can handle." (Well, I am angry with God right now and wondering what on earth he was thinking! I am way past what I can handle!)

☐ "_____ would have been healed if you or _____ had more faith." (I'd like to smack you upside the head!)

☐ "I'LL BE IN TOUCH." (I HEAR
GOODBYE IN YOUR VOICE.)

☐ "YOUR MOTHER/FATHER WAS OLD AND OLD PEOPLE
ARE SUPPOSED TO DIE." (THAT DOESN'T MEAN I AM
NOT SUPPOSED TO GRIEVE OR MISS HIM/HER!)

It is important to remember that the intention of most people is not to irritate us or to harm us in anyway. Many people speak without thinking. Many times people are nervous and don't know what to say. Others view themselves as full of "wisdom"— "wisdom" they feel they need to share. Even someone with a similar death experience is capable of saying something annoying.

Decide in advance that if someone says something awful, hurtful, insulting or just plain stupid, that you will shake the words off and forgive them. Do not allow yourself to get stuck in a "pothole" by allowing the words or the incident to play over and over again in your mind. Find a few good friends to share the incident with and shake those words with fangs off until they fall off for good!

A Gem of Hope:

There is wisdom in deciding in advance that you will not let the words that people say offend you. Because once you have made this decision, when someone does say something offensive to you, you'll have already prepared yourself in advance to ignore the words with fangs. This shift in thinking is pro-active and will enable you to let go of the words more easily.

The Destination Is Healing: Action Step

Make a gratitude list. Write down the name of each family member and friend that you are thankful for and why.

_____

_____

_____

_____

_____

_____

_____

_____

_____

_____

_____

_____

_____

_____

_____

_____

_____

_____

_____

_____

_____

_____

SPECIAL DAYS AND HOLIDAYS

SPECIAL DAYS AND HOLIDAYS ARRIVE WHETHER WE WANT THEM TO OR NOT

But those who hope in the LORD will renew their strength. They will soar on wings like eagles, they will run and not grow weary, they will walk and not faint.

(Isaiah 40:31)

Do you find yourself sometimes coasting along, doing pretty well, and then you realize that a holiday or special day is coming up? And, all of a sudden you find yourself experiencing bursts of grief and unexpected anxiety. It may be a birthday, anniversary, or milestone such as a graduation. Maybe it's a family wedding that you are dreading. If your parent or child has died, Mother's Day and Father's Day can be difficult.

Following the death of a loved one, it is very common for the anticipation of holidays and special days to stir up emotions, particularly feelings of sadness, dread, fear and anxiety. Sometimes this difficult period of anticipation can start a week, a few weeks or even a month before the day arrives. It is also not unusual to be exhausted for a few days after the holiday or special day. What about the day itself?

> The anticipation of the day in question is almost always worse than the actual day itself.

Special days and holidays arrive whether we want them to or not. The majority of the time the anticipation and anxiety that we experience leading up to the day is worse than what the actual day brings. This is important to remember when the pain of grief is raw and surviving means being proud of yourself for just getting out of bed, getting dressed, and being able to attend to necessary daily tasks and responsibilities. Add in shopping for presents, attending family functions, coming up with costumes and everything else that goes along with holidays and special days—well, it can be overwhelming!

A season or special time of year that was important to your relationship with your loved one can also produce bursts of grief. Sometimes this is confusing because we experience intense waves of grief and can't figure out why. Later we realize that a special day, holiday or a new season is about to arrive or has already passed by. It is not unusual for the mind to block out the fact that a special day or season of year is on the horizon. At the same time it is normal to experience the heart sending out grief infused messages creating more intense waves of grief than normal. These continue until we are emotionally ready to remember.

Linda shares:

> I was feeling out of sorts and experiencing strange waves of intense grief bursts the spring after Donald died. It took me a few weeks to figure out that the arrival of spring itself was the problem. For the first time, Donald would not be around to plant a garden with me. I had to grieve this loss also.

Sometimes, different friends and family members try to keep us from grieving during these special times. This is why it's important to remember that stuffing emotions is not healthy or healing. On these important days, you need to surround yourself with supportive people. Let the tears flow. You need to talk about your loved one. Family members and friends also need the freedom to cry and to talk about the deceased.

Many times others don't realize that a special day is coming up for us. Sometimes we have to tell them. It is also helpful to keep in mind that these days are not only painful for us, but they are painful for our children, other family members, and friends. And, the day that pushes your emotional buttons and produces more grief for you to deal with may not be the same day that pushes another family member's emotional buttons.

It is helpful and healing to be mindful of each family member's unique stress and anxiety level on special days and holidays, too. Respecting each other's need to grieve by listening and showing support promotes healing. Since grief work is exhausting, reduce the pressure and stress by tailoring activities to your energy level. It's important to remember:

- You don't need to accept every invitation.

- It's okay to decide not to send out as many Christmas cards or not to send out any Christmas cards at all.

- It's okay not to do as much shopping.

- It's okay not to decorate as much or not to decorate at all.

- It's okay not to want to cook.

- It's okay to allow yourself to make the necessary changes without burdening yourself with unnecessary guilt.

A Gem of Hope:

Eating healthy food, hydrating with water, and fitting in naps reduces special day and holiday stress. Eat well, drink water and fit in some naps.

The Destination Is Healing: Action Step

If you need to cry, call the friend that will allow you to cry. If you need to laugh, call the friend who can make you laugh. If you need to "escape," call the friend who will take you out. If you don't feel like you want to get out of bed, call the friend that motivates you.

THE IMPORTANCE OF
HAVING A PLAN

"Do not let what you cannot do interfere with what you can do."

Coach John Wooden

Planning can be difficult because when we are grieving we don't always like to make decisions or plan anything in advance, but we need to. Without a plan, the risk of being completely miserable and feeling depressed on a special day or holiday is usually 100-percent guaranteed.

The creative work of planning helps everyone involved to re-focus raw grief energy into something positive. Planning also inspires forward-moving thinking, which is healing. If possible, involve your children in the planning process. A plan also provides structure. Structure helps with mental focus and emotional balance. Structure is just as important for grieving adults as it is for grieving children.

When you plan for the day it is also important to have a back-up plan. A back-up plan gives you another option in the event that you change your mind about the first plan. And, it's okay to change your mind. It's also okay to give yourself even another option, plan number three, which is deciding last minute to do nothing at all. Deciding that you don't want to do anything at all happens sometimes.

This is fine, unless children are involved. When children are involved it is necessary to consider how the change will impact them. Sometimes it means we have to stick to the original plan no matter what we personally feel like doing or not doing.

When making your plan, you need to decide if you want to do things differently or the same. Some people do things the same. However, many people find that doing things differently helps. Sometimes it is just too painful to try to maintain something that just can't ever be the same. Unfortunately, making needed changes is sometimes difficult. Change many times triggers opposition from a few or all family members.

If young children, teenagers or young adults are involved, it may be necessary to stick with some of your traditions. Younger people (and sometimes older ones) very often expect things to be the way they always were. This means it is necessary for everyone to communicate honestly. Never assume. Ask. You need to share what you can and can't handle. It is also important to allow others to share what they can and can't handle. Everyone's feelings need to be considered.

Even when we are so worn out from grief that we don't feel like talking, communicating with our loved ones is necessary because it helps to eliminate unnecessary stressors for us and for them. Communicating helps everyone establish *reasonable expectations*. Unmet expectations cause relationship problems. Promoting healing and building relationships is the ultimate goal, even when it comes to figuring out what to do on special days and holidays.

You need to:

- Involve your children in the planning.

- Set healthy boundaries.

- Negotiate.

- Compromise.

- Occasionally, it is necessary to make a decision independent of other family members for the good of everyone involved. This happens sometimes when children are involved. If you find yourself in this type of situation, it is advisable to let each child know in advance what the change is. For instance, if you decide you do not want to stay home for Christmas and you think taking the family to Florida is an excellent idea, you might be surprised by the resistance that arises even against a wonderful opportunity.

- Change is difficult for each of us. But young children and especially teenagers tend to resist change, just because every change right now is something else the child can't control. And teenagers detest surprises. Planning together as a family eliminates the extra parental stress that comes from parenting disappointed, angry, grieving children.

- Be prepared for special day and holiday emotional surprises, too. It is not uncommon to be shocked by the stressful response that a previously non-eventful holiday produces. By non-eventful, we mean a holiday that really did not hold any prior significant meaning.

Linda shares:

> I remember ignoring the arrival of Memorial Day weekend the first year after Donald died. We never did anything special on this weekend as a couple or as a family. Boy was I sorry I didn't plan anything. I was miserable. My children were miserable. From that day on—even now—I always have a special day/holiday plan.

Sometimes trying to come up with a different plan is difficult. Are you wondering what you can change? Are you concerned about how it will work out? It helps to keep in mind that making changes on special days and holidays does not mean that you are forgetting about your loved one. Making changes does not mean forever forgetting old traditions. Having fun and laughing is not a sign of forgetting either. Healing is what is happening.

It is also important to understand that what you do the first year on a special day or holiday may not be what you decide to do the next year. Establishing new traditions that work for you and for your family usually takes a few times of trying out different ideas before one clicks.

SOME EXAMPLES OF CHANGES THAT YOU CAN MAKE ARE:

- Change where you have the meal. It can be someone else's "turn" to host the dinner. For those of you who have always done the cooking, this could be a real treat. You'll get to actually be in on the conversation rather than in the kitchen.

- Go out to eat.
- Change the time the meal is served.
- Change the seating arrangement at the table.
- Have a barbecue instead of your typical holiday meal.
- Serve a buffet rather than the usual sit down dinner.
- Change the location. Take a trip/vacation.
- Travel and visit friends or family.

HONOR YOUR LOVED ONE ON THESE OCCASIONS BY:

- Wrapping something that belonged to your loved one up: a special keepsake. Give it to another grieving family member or special friend who loves and misses your loved one.
- Making a donation to your church or special charity in honor of your loved one.
- For his/her birthday ask people to send you a "memory" or favorite picture of your loved one.
- Watching videos and sharing pictures. Tell the stories behind the videos and pictures.
- Doing something in memory or in honor of your loved one that he or she liked to do. Invite others to join you.

A Gem of Hope:

Oftentimes after the first year, the people in your life expect you to be "over it." We are never "over it." But, the experience that most of us have had is that we do eventually enjoy special days and holidays and the arrival of different seasons again. These days will become sweet for you again, too, just in a new and different way.

The Destination Is Healing: Action Step

Decide today to undertake new activities. Decide today to create new holiday and special day rituals that include ways to maintain the memory of your loved one in a healthy way. Doing so is part of healing and also is part of finding your "New Normal."

THE
ANNIVERSARY
OF THE DEATH

When I am pressed on every side by troubles, I am not crushed and broken. When I am perplexed because I don't know why things happen as they do, I don't give up and quit.

(2 Corinthians 4:8, TLB)

Any day that is a day that you used to look forward to can produce pain now that your loved one has died. But what about the day that was never part of your special days until now, what about the first anniversary of the death?

The first anniversary of the death is a milestone. You will have lived through every special day and holiday, all four seasons—365 days—one whole year, without your loved one. The anticipation of this day usually produces enormous emotional and physical responses. Always have a plan for the day.

Possible plans:

- Take the day off of work.

- Dinner and a movie alone.

- Dinner and a movie with family or friends. Before or after dinner each person can share a special memory.

- Spend time at the cemetery.

- Hold a memorial service. Light a candle. Each person can share a special memory.

- Watch videos or look at pictures.

- Meet with family and friends and share stories.

- Go to church.

- Make a donation to your church or favorite charity in honor of your loved one.

- Plant a tree or bush.

- Go to the zoo.

It is also very important that you take time on this day to remember how much *you* have accomplished during the first 365 days. Be proud of yourself!

It is also normal to be exhausted for a few days or even a few weeks after a special day or holiday passes. The first anniversary of the death is no exception. Eat healthy food, hydrate with water and take the time to rest.

Each year the anniversary of the death will be a little different because each year you will be at a different point in your healing. What you want and need to do on this day each year will probably change, too.

A Gem of Hope:

The anticipation of the anniversary of the death is usually worse than the actual day itself.

The Destination Is Healing: Action Step

Pamper yourself. Schedule a relaxation massage with a licensed massage therapist. Touch is healing.

MY PERSONAL HOLIDAY PLAN

"The real voyage of discovery consists not in seeking new landscapes, but in having new eyes."

Marcel Proust

Many times it's beneficial to sit down and write out a holiday plan. This is one way to review and remember the past
and at the same time to plan a future that remembers the
past and your loved one. The following plan, will help you
to organize your thoughts, and your holiday or special day.

1. I predict that the most painful parts of this holiday sea-
    son for me will be:

2. The most difficult people to be with might be:

3. My grief triggers will be:

4. Words that would be helpful for me to hear would be:

5. My support people (those who can hear my grief) are:

6. Last year or years prior to my loss I celebrated this holi-
    day by:

7. This year I want to include or exclude the following
    traditions:

8. What considerations do I need to make for my children
    or grandchildren?

A Gem of Hope:

Most people find that they do enjoy holidays and special days again, just in a new and different way.

The Destination Is Healing: Action Step

Think about or write out your plan for the next upcoming holiday or special day.

_____

_____

_____

_____

_____

_____

_____

_____

_____

_____

_____

_____

_____

_____

_____

_____

_____

FINDING A "NEW NORMAL"

THE FUTURE LOOKS QUITE DIFFERENT AT EACH "ROAD MARKER" ALONG THE WAY

"The best thing about the future is it only comes one day at a time."

Abraham Lincoln

What you'll notice as you're traveling down the path of grief, doing your grief work, working through the pain, and courageously pushing forward into the future is this: the future looks quite different at each "road marker" along the way and many times, the phases overlap for a period of time. How does the future look different?

- During the "Numbness or Shock Phase" it's common to feel that there is no future. Feeling empty is normal.

- Then we get to the "Painful/Disorientation Phase" and it hurts so bad that we sometimes hope and pray there isn't a future, at least not anything like what we are experiencing at this point in the grief process.

- During the "Realization and Readjustment Phase" the possibility of a future seems possible.

- Finally, we reach the "Reestablishment Phase" and we begin to believe that there is a future. We know the future will be different, and maybe even good!

Many times we try to side-step dealing with our emotional pain as we travel along the path of grief, but we still expect to arrive at the next "road marker" ready for the next "healing" step. Understandably, many people want to hurry toward the period of "Readjustment," bypassing some of the early twists, turns and necessary grief work because it hurts and they don't want to go through the pain.

What we discover is that unresolved grief pain always finds us again and haunts us until we make the choice to work through it and to resolve it. There is no way to walk over the pain, under the pain, around the pain or to run from it or ahead of it. Each griever must walk through the pain, process the pain and then let go of the pain. *The reality is that it is not until we arrive at the "Readjustment Phase," having done our grief work, that we're ready to let go of the pain.* You will not be able to let go of the pain if you are still in shock, numb, in pain much of the time, and holding on to anger and guilt.

However, eventually you will arrive at the "Readjust-ment Phase." If you arrive at this "road marker," and you have successfully dealt with everything along the way, especially your emotions, you'll be ready for the work of "Readjustment."

A Gem of Hope:

"Anywhere with Jesus I can safely go; Anywhere he leads me in this world below...Anywhere with Jesus I am not alone; Other friends may fail me, He is still my own; Though His hand may lead me over dreary ways...Anywhere with Jesus I am not afraid." [30]

Jessie B. Pounds 1887

The Destination Is Healing: Action Step

"Sometimes your grief can be so overwhelming because it encompasses the grieving you never did for other, earlier losses in your life. Let yourself feel the pain of those losses too."

Karen Katafiasz, Grief Therapy [31]

LETTING GO OF THE PAIN DOES NOT MEAN FORGETTING: READJUSTMENT

"Behold the turtle. He makes progress only when he sticks his neck out."

James Bryant Conant

Some people get as far as the "Readjustment Phase" and find themselves stuck. They get stuck because they can't let go of the pain. Letting go of the pain is tough! Some people equate letting go to forgetting—but it's not that at all! One widowed woman at a New Hope Center for Grief Support group said, "If I stop feeling miserable, people would think I didn't care about my husband."

The feelings that this woman expressed are normal. But the reality is, once you've worked through the pain and dealt with your deep emotions, you realize that letting go of the pain is the next natural step along the path of grief. The arrival at the "road marker" of "Readjustment" signals that it's time to make the choice to decide to let go of the pain and to begin to find ways to keep your loved one's memory alive.

Your loved one will always be with you because you'll place him/her in a special place in your heart, forever and always. Letting go of the pain does not mean forgetting your loved one. However, sometimes we can't let go of the pain because we are stuck in the grief process. So how do you know if you are stuck? Can you find yourself on the list below?

☐ IF IT'S BEEN TWO YEARS OR MORE SINCE YOU LOVED ONE DIED AND YOU'RE STILL ACTIVELY GRIEVING.

☐ IF IT'S BEEN TWO YEARS OR MORE AND YOU HAVEN'T BEGUN TO GET RID OF ANY OF HIS/HER BELONGINGS.

☐ IF YOU FIND YOURSELF OBSESSING ABOUT A PARTICULAR ASPECT OF YOUR LOVED ONE'S DEATH. FOR EXAMPLE, MAYBE YOU'RE STILL ANGRY WITH SOMEONE BECAUSE HE OR SHE DIDN'T COME TO THE FUNERAL. OR MAYBE THE DOCTOR MISSED AN IMPORTANT SYMPTOM AND YOU ARE UNABLE TO FORGIVE.

When we realize that we are stuck, we need to address the area or areas that we are stuck in. Many times though, the problem is that we're just not sure if we are ready to begin letting go. How do you know when you're ready to begin the "letting go" process? Let's start by identifying when you're *not* ready to let go. You're not ready to "let go" until you've dealt with your early grief and many of the "firsts." Find yourself on the following list. I have dealt with:

☐   THE FIRST TIME I'VE GONE TO A FAMILIAR PLACE WITHOUT MY LOVED ONE.

☐   THE FIRST BIRTHDAY. (MY LOVED ONE'S BIRTHDAY/MY BIRTHDAY WITHOUT HIM/HER)

☐   THE FIRST WEDDING ANNIVERSARY.

☐   THE FIRST ANNIVERSARY OF THE DEATH.

☐   THE FIRST YEAR OF HOLIDAYS AND SPECIAL DAYS.

☐   THE FIRST FOUR SEASONS SINCE THE DEATH.

Now let's assume you've dealt with the pain and the emotions and are at this place in your grief journey where you're ready to "let go of the pain." What do you need to do?

> You need to make a conscious choice to "let go of the pain." You didn't have a choice in your loss, but you do have a choice as to how you're going to go on. This choice can be in the form of a question: "Do I hold on to the grief and the pain that goes with it, or do I begin to let go and to make the choice to look ahead to a future without my loved one?

You may feel like you're caught in the middle of a battle— the battle between the "pull of the past" and your desire to be happy. This "pull of the past" involves holding on to what was comfortable and safe and living in the past, while the other option can lead to a potentially happy future. But there's a catch: It includes dealing with what's unfamiliar.

This includes:

- Trying/risking new things.
- Taking chances.

Elizabeth Neeld, in her book, *Seven Choices,* calls this a time of "Reconstruction." She shares:

> Reconstruction...is a time of groping and stumbling, of not knowing yet taking a step forward anyway, of making changes without any certainty of achieving a good outcome. It's a time when we are beginning to think about goals and dreams for the future but often have very little clarity about how those goals and dreams can be accomplished.[32]

Others have referred to this as a transitional time. A time in which you go from who you were to who you'll become. It's normal to decide that it is time to begin the process of "letting go" and at the same time be unclear about what it is that you are supposed to let go of. Just what is it that you need to let go of?

1. You need to begin to let go of your loved one's thing if you haven't already. This is a big step in the "letting go" process. Re-visit chapter four, *The Belongings.*

2. You need to "let go" of what was comfortable and normal. Eventually, you'll discover a "New Normal." Our lives were "comfortable" with the relationship we had with the person who died. Much of our self-identity and purpose was wrapped up in that relationship. Because of this, many of us struggle with self-worth and self-identity at this time. A few examples of self identity issues are:

- Loss of parent: You may now be the "older generation." Your parent(s) may have always been there for you. You went to him/her/both for advice.

- Loss of child: Did you live through this child and his/her accomplishments? Many parents do.

- Loss of spouse: Many feel they're only half a person. No longer are you Mr. or Mrs. "We" becomes "I."

- Was the person who died the only one who gave you unconditional love? Were you quite dependent on him/her?

3. You need to "let go" of dreams and future plans with the person who died. These need to be replaced with new goals, dreams, future plans. For example:

- If your spouse died, you might want to change your retirement plans.

- If your child died, instead of looking at his/her future and how it would involve you, begin looking at yourself. Set some new goals for yourself, make some positive plans.

4. You need to let go of your anger. Especially anger toward God.

   • Letting go and moving on is not possible if you're holding on to unresolved anger or if you're unable to forgive.

5. If you're stuck in the "anger mode," seek outside help to get you through it.

The last question you need to ask yourself is, "Am I ready to take control of my life?" In the early stages of grief, it's easier to give up control and become dependent on others for support and help with decision making. The desire and need to take back control and responsibility of our life allows us to move forward and begin the process of purposefully entering the "Reestablishment Phase."

Eventually, each griever needs to make a choice. "Do I choose to live or do I choose to only exist? If you make the choice to hold on to the grief and the pain it represents, you've made the choice to simply 'exist.' You can do this and become a lifelong mourner. But if you know people who have done this, and some people do choose this existence, it's not a purposeful, fulfilling existence. Instead, your choice should be to 'live.' In order to do this you will need to give yourself permission to stop grieving. This is not an easy process, but it is necessary.

A Gem of Hope:

"The great thing in the world is not so much where we stand as in what direction we are moving."

Oliver Wendell Holmes

The Destination Is Healing: Action Step

Sometimes we need to say goodbye not only to our loved one, but to life as we knew and understood it before the death happened. Remember this is not forgetting, this is relinquishing the past. Write a letter expressing your feelings about "letting go." Talk to his/her picture. When you say good-bye, acknowledge that you're no longer going to share your life with your loved one. Acknowledge that you're going to *live* in spite of the death.

THE WORK OF REESTABLISHMENT

"And the trouble is, if you don't risk anything, you risk even more."

Erica Jong

After a period of "Readjustment" and figuring out what you personally need to do to let go of the pain, it's normal to start wondering, "Where do I go from here?" The answer is to continue walking forward along the path of grief until you arrive at the road marker of "Reestablishment." "Reestablishment" hinges on acceptance and reconciliation. The definition of "reconcile" is *to accept something not desired.*

"Accepting" a death is different than "getting over" a death. This is why we do not use the word "recover," which implies one should just be able to "get over" the death of a loved one. Doing the work of grief eventually allows us to become reconciled to the fact that our loved one or loved ones are dead. Slowly, we accept what we did not desire, and we also accept or become reconciled to all the changes and secondary losses that accompany death.

There are certain things that you need to do in order to move forward in a healthy way. The following "checklist" will help you determine where you are. Find yourself.

☐ I'VE DECIDED TO LET GO OF THE PAIN.
THIS INCLUDES DEALING WITH MY
ANGER AND GUILT FEELINGS.

☐ I'VE GOTTEN RID OF THE "LINKING OBJECTS"
AND I AM HOLDING ON TO THE "MEMENTOS."

- If there was a room that was "his," it's now "yours."

- Those mementos bring you comfort rather than lots of tears.

☐ I'VE LET GO OF WHAT WAS
COMFORTABLE AND NORMAL.

- You understand that things can't be the same and that you need to continue to create your "New Normal."

- You've begun to establish a new "Self-Identity."

- Maybe you've even made the decision to move to a new house that is "yours."

☐ I'VE LET GO OF THE HOPES, DREAMS, AND
FUTURE PLANS THAT INCLUDED MY LOVED
ONE AND I HAVE REPLACED THEM WITH NEW
HOPES, DREAMS AND FUTURE PLANS.

- The future may begin to look hopeful and possible. This might include planning a future in whatever way that might mean for you: by making educational plans, volunteering for a worthwhile cause, etc. In the early stages of your grief, all you could or should do was take one day at a time. Now you are able to look toward the future, and you may even begin to make retirement plans.

☐ THE INTENSE SORROW AND PAIN I ONCE FELT DOESN'T SEEM TO BE THERE ANYMORE. INSTEAD I FEEL A MILD SADNESS.

☐ I AM BEGINNING TO LOOK FORWARD TO THE HOLIDAYS AGAIN.

☐ I'M SMILING A LOT MORE. I CAN EVEN LAUGH AND NOT FEEL GUILTY.

☐ I'VE BECOME MORE INTERESTED IN THE WORLD AND IN INCREASING MY ACTIVITY LEVEL.

☐ I'M BEGINNING TO FEEL GOOD ABOUT MYSELF AND EVEN THE WAY I LOOK AGAIN.

☐ I AM BEGINNING TO RECOGNIZE MY STRENGTHS.

☐ I HAVE STOPPED FEELING ENVIOUS OF OTHERS' HAPPINESS. I NOW FIND MYSELF CELEBRATING WITH THEM.

☐   I REALIZE THAT I AM NOW FUNCTIONING AT THE CAPACITY I WAS FUNCTIONING AT BEFORE MY LOVED ONE DIED. MY MEMORY IS BACK AND I CAN MAKE PLANS AGAIN.

☐   I CAN MAKE DECISIONS AGAIN!

☐   I KNOW I WILL SURVIVE.

Once you've done these things, you can begin to move forward in life without the "physical" presence of the person who has died.

- This involves detaching yourself from the emotional ties you had to that person.

- Your relationship with the person who died will be different now: No longer a physical relationship, but one of memory.

- You've begun to move into a new way of life without forgetting the old.

You'll need to begin to reinvest the emotional energy that was invested in the person who died into other relationships or activities that will give you emotional satisfaction and fulfillment.

Some examples:

- New friendships—making new friends is risking. Sometimes it means rejection. Are you ready for that?

- Volunteer work.

- New job.

- Taking classes/maybe finishing your degree.

One of the biggest obstacles that keeps people from choosing to "Move On" is the fear that their loved one will be forgotten. It's up to you to make sure that doesn't happen. There are things that you can do to keep your loved one's memory alive. A few examples:

- Display pictures and other mementos.

- Make donations to charitable organizations in his/her name.

- Light a candle at the holidays.

- Every spring or fall plant a tree.

This is the time when many people get to a point where they find a new or renewed relationship with God, in many cases stronger than it was before the death. Have you felt like you have been held captive by your grief?

> You will seek me and find me when you seek me with all your heart. I will be found by you, declares the Lord, and will bring you back from captivity.
>
> (Jeremiah 29:13–14)

A Gem of Hope:

For I know the plans I have for you, declares the
LORD...plans to give you hope and a future.

(Jeremiah 29:11)

The Destination Is
Healing: Action Step

Ask God to help you. He has not deserted you. You just
need to call out to him.

"NEW BEGINNINGS"

"What a new face courage puts on everything!"

Ralph Waldo Emerson

It takes great courage to step out into the unknown and begin the process of creating personal "New Beginnings." It's easier and more comfortable many times to just sit back and watch the world go by. That is, until we slowly begin to realize that we are going to miss out on the healing that can only come from *engaging* in life once again.

You will intuitively know when you are ready, willing and able to begin *actively* pursuing "New Beginnings." How will you know? You will suddenly become aware that you are standing right in the middle of an intersection that each of us who has gone before you has stood in. It is the intersection of "Life Long Mourner" and "Triumphant Survivor."[33] Only you can decide which direction to go in. Sadly, not everyone is going to travel the path of grief successfully and become "Triumphant Survivors." It's a choice.

The words "fearless" and "courage" come to mind many times when we find it necessary to consider something new or to make some type of change. Most of us desire to live "fearless" and "courageous" lives. Unfortunately, this is not a time when many of us feel particularly courageous and fearless. This is actually a time in healing that requires many of us to decide that it will be necessary to start doing new things and making necessary changes, even when we are afraid.

Even when the desire of your heart is to be a "Triumphant Survivor," it's still normal to experience an emotional battle between the "pull of the past," fear, and the desire to be happy again. Sometimes applying the "Nuts with This!" principle helps.

Linda shares:

> About a year after Donald's death I had a conversation with my neighbor that re-directed my thinking and ultimately my healing. We were discussing how much we both missed Donald, and my friend shared a bit of her mother's story with me. I had only briefly met her mother on a few occasions. The only thing that I knew about her mother up until this point was that she was a very nice, outgoing woman.
>
> My friend shared with me that day that her mother was also a widow. One day about a year after the death of her husband and actively working on her grief, she telephoned her daughter (my friend) and told her that she had decided, "*Nuts With This*." She didn't want to cling to the past and pain and "do this" anymore. She didn't want to constantly think about "it" anymore. She was ready to step back into life again.

My friend went on to explain that every time her mother felt the need to re-direct her thinking in a positive manner, she would tell herself *"Nuts With This,"* I'm finding something new, positive and productive to do today."

And, she did. Her mother lived a very full and *adventurous* life until her death a few years ago. After her *"Nuts With This"* revelation she joined a singles group at a local church, traveled, and was a wonderful and encouraging friend to many. After working through the grief process, healing and finding peace and contentment in living alone as a single person, she eventually did meet someone. By this time she knew, "beyond a shadow of a doubt," that she was ready for the "work" of merging her life with the life of someone else. This woman had *"Nuts With This"* courage that was to be admired. Those three words— *"Nuts With This"*— stuck in my brain like glue on a stick. Those three words became my mantra. Every time I felt depressed, scared, angry, unsure, etc., I would think about this woman's courage and I too would decide once again, *"Nuts With This."* I'm finding something new and productive to do today." Some days I found myself continuously saying *"Nuts With This."* However, I was also at a point where knew that if I didn't start "creating a new life" for myself, I would die.

Many times "New Beginning" opportunities present themselves even while we are still trying to figure out what happened to us and what happened to the life that we knew and understood before the death occurred. If you can embrace these new opportunities when they present, you will find that purpose, direction, healing and even more life changing opportunities follow. Sometimes it is helpful to hear about how others have embraced the challenge and the process of finding a "New Normal" and healing at the same time.

Cathy shares:

> Do you remember the gentleman I told you about—the one who lined up his wife's shoes on the dining room table? (chapter four: "The Dining Room Table Plan") This wonderful man was married for fifty-one years to the "love of his life." They didn't have a lot of friends, just a small family.
>
> A few months after his wife died, one of his daughters brought him to a grief support group that I was leading. He came up to me at the end of the first session and said, "Cathy, you don't know what you're talking about. I was doing fine until I came here tonight." Apparently, things had come up that night that he thought he had dealt with but hadn't—or he was avoiding thinking about them. Because he was the type of man who finished what he started, he finished the series and told me on the last night that he was glad he did. He went on to get involved in one of our on-going groups for widows and widowers and made several friends through the group.

After a period of time, he made his home available to me to hold grief support groups. He made the coffee and dessert. I just facilitated the group! It was a great arrangement. Through the on-going group and the many groups I held in his home, many people grew to care about this man and call him "friend." When he turned eighty, his daughters threw a surprise birthday party for him. Do you know there were almost eighty people at that party? More than half of the people attending were people he met after his wife's death through his involvement with the many grief support groups he attended and hosted.

Getting involved in a grief support group has many benefits. As you get to know others, share your story and listen to others share, you realize that you are not alone. You also realize that what you're experiencing is normal for grief.

Linda Shares:

Three months ago, I was contacted by one of my parents' friends. He lives a thousand miles away from me, so we have been keeping up by telephone. His wife died suddenly four months ago. After talking with him a few times, I sent him a copy of the manuscript of this book. He called this past week to tell me that he is telling his "story" to everyone he meets and it is working. He is slowly experiencing healing and in the process, he is meeting many other people who need to tell their story and to be heard. He also went to the doctor and to his surprise found out his blood pressure is high due to grief stress. He is now taking medication.

My friend is also attending two different support grief groups, and he rescued a dog from his local animal shelter. Involving himself in these activities has given him the opportunity to share his story, listen to others share and to learn as much as he can about the grief process. The companionship of his pet is comforting.

It occurred to him while he was telling his story to "anyone" willing to listen, that he has many friends who are grieving and who are unfortunately homebound due to old age/health issues. This dear man decided to routinely start visiting each of his homebound friends, with the goal of allowing each friend the healing opportunity to find the words, speak the words of his/her grief story and to be heard. He is also sharing what he is learning about the grief process with each friend. A "ministry" was born out of his desire to share what he is leaning and to help others. Purpose and healing are found when we grab hold of the "hands" of someone else that is grieving and walk the path together.

A Gem of Hope:

When we are willing to do our part, even if it means making changes and doing new things "afraid," we not only build confidence, but also move closer to the destination of healing, acceptance and new beginnings.

The Destination is Healing: Action Step

Join a grief support group—or join three. Attend each group simultaneously or stagger attending different groups over the first few years. Grief work and healing are a process.

CHOICES

"It was not your choice to travel down the path of grief. But, you do have a choice as to how you respond."

Cathy Clough

Choices—we all need to make them. Each choice we make has a consequence: positive, negative, or neutral. Even when we avoid or delay making a necessary choice, we are making a decision that has consequences. Choices move us forward emotionally or keep us stuck.

After losing someone you love deeply, someone who was an important part of your life, you eventually get to a place where it is time to move on and make a new life without that person or you can make the choice to live in the past, focusing on the way things used to be and what will never be again. Sadly, some people decide to live in the past.

Fortunately, you can choose to become a "Triumphant Survivor" early on in your grief. However, it's hard to actually start a new way of life until you've done your grief work. So, if you are reading this and you're still pretty new at grief, start practicing the following behaviors, but don't try to rush through your grief too quickly. Trying to move too quickly will only overwhelm you. In addition, what we all learn is that there is no way to move through the grief process at a high rate of speed, because the grief process is a "low-gear" experience and process due to the fact that there is so much to process emotionally.

HEALING CHOICES:

Choice #1: Choose to put your loved one in a special place in your heart, drawing on the memories, but not living for them. This is a process.

Choice #2: Choose to be happy. You can go around with a smile on your face or a frown. Smiles are contagious and will draw people to you. However, in the beginning season of grief, most of us have a hard time locating our smile. Keep looking for it until you find it again.

Choice # 3: Choose to be your own person. Find out you who you are without your loved one, not as his or her wife, parent, child, etc. Think of this as a time of self discovery. This is also a process.

Choice #4: Choose to like who you are becoming or who you've become. Be your own best friend. Spend time alone and learn to be comfortable with yourself. If you're comfortable with you, chances are other people will be comfortable with you also.

Choice #5: Choose to make new friends.

We all need friends to do things with and to grow with. A good grief support group is a great place to make new friends who share a similar experience.

Choice #6: Choose to find words that define your feelings of grief and to speak those words aloud. Share your story with others.

Choice #7: Choose to continue to learn about the grief process.

Choice #8: Choose to do your personal grief work.

A Gem of Hope:

There is a future out there for you. You may not know what it entails or how you're going to find it, but God does. Allow him to guide you and get you there.

The Destination Is Healing: Action Step

The choices that you make as you journey along the path of grief will determine the direction that you take and the outcome. When contemplating a choice, focus on the desired result: reaching the destination of healing, acceptance and new beginnings. Will the choice you are considering get you there? Try making at least one choice everyday that moves you forward toward this goal.

Our hope is that you will choose healing.

ENDNOTES

Introduction

1   Daniel Siegel, *The Developing Mind* (Guilford Press, 1999) 296 & 297

2   Victoria Alexander, *In The Wake of Suicide* (San Francisco: Jossey-Bass Web Publishers, 1991): Introduction

3   Lindemann, Eric, psychiatrist and grief expert, coined the phrase "*Grief Work*" in 1944.

Finding The Words That I Need

4   *Chambers Synonyms and Antonyms*, (2004)

5   *Merriam Webster's Collegiate Dictionary*, 10th ed., (1996)

Common Reactions To Grief

6   Daniel Siegel, *The Developing Mind* (Guilford Press, 1999); 296 & 297

7   Hospice of Michigan, *Reactions to Grief*, www.hospiceofmichigangriefreactions, (Retrieved 6/12/09)

8   Cathy Clough, *From Grief to New Hope Facilitators Guide*, (2002):9

The Need to Speak My Words
of Grief Out Loud

9   Daniel J. Siegel, *The Mindful Brain* (W.W. Norton & Co., New York-London, 2007) Citing research (Oshner, Bunge, Gross & Gabrieli, 2002): 224

10   Dr. Caroline Leaf, *Who Switched Off My Brain* (Dr Leaf Switch On Your Brain, 2007):15

The Need To Know That I Have Been Heard

11   Karen Katafiasz, *Grief Therapy* (One Caring Place, Abby Press, 1993):26

The Danger In Stuffing Emotions

12   Don Colbert, M.D., *Deadly Emotions* (Thomas Nelson Publishers, Nashville, 2003):53

13   Dr Caroline Leaf, *Who Switched Off My Brain* (Dr. Leaf Switch On Your Brain, 2007):7

14   Candace B. Pert, PhD., *Molecules of Emotion* (Scribner, 1230 Avenue of Americas, New York, NY 10020, 1997):273

15   Dr. Caroline Leaf, (Appearance on Enjoying Everyday Life, 2/15/10)

Tears Contain The Miracle of Healing

16   Jerry Bergman, "*The Miracle of Tears*" Creation 15 (4): 16–18, September 1993, Http://www.answersingenesis.org/creation/v15/i4/tears.asp Retrieved 9/16/09

Defining a Pitfall and a Pothole

17   *Merriam Webster's Collegiate Dictionary*, 10th ed. , (1996)

Should read: The Importance of Monitoring
Your Thoughts as Healing Occurs

18   Joe Dispenza, D.C., *Evolve Your Brain*, (Health communications, Inc. 3201 S.W. 15th Street, Deerfield Beach, Fl 33442–8190, 2007):43

Momentos and Linking Items:
Its All a Matter of Perception

19   Dr. Vamik Volkan, *Pathological Grief*, 1972, 1973.

But...I'm Not Angry

20   Gary Chapman, *Anger, Handling a Powerful Emotion In A Healthy Way*, (Northfield Publishing, 215 West Locust Street, Chicago, Il 60610,1999,2007):29

Identifying the Stranglehold of Anger

21   Don Colbert, M.D. *Deadly Emotions* (Thomas Nelson Publishers, Nashville, 2003):37

22   Don Colbert, M.D. *Deadly Emotions*-Chapter 5

23   Gary Chapman, *Anger-Handling A Powerful Emotion In A Healthy Way*: 21,23

The 4-A's of Anger *(Used by Permission)*

24 Edgar N. Jackson, *The Many Faces of Grief*, (Parthenon Press, Abingdon/Nashville, Tennessee, United States of America, 1972, 1973,1974,1975 ,1976,1977):18,19

25 Edgar Jackson, *The Many Faces of Grief*:19

Forgiveness

26 Lewis B. Smedes, *Forgive and Forget: Healing the Hurts We Don't Deserve* (HarperCollins Publishers, 1984):38

27 Don Colbert, M.D., *Deadly Emotions:*163

Normal Grief Depression

28 Edgar Jackson, *The Many Faces of Grief*:67

29 Helpguide.org/mental/grief/complicated_grief_mourning_or_bereavement.htm-,AmericanCancerSociety, Retrieved 12/10/09

Changes In Friendships

30 Daniel Siegel, *The Developing Mind*: 296 &297

The Future Looks Different At Each Road Marker Along The Way

31 Jessie B. Pounds, *Anywhere With Jesus*(Hymn 1887)

32 Karen Katafiasz, *Grief Therapy*:25

Letting Go Of The Pain Does Not
Mean Forgetting: Readjustment

33 Elizabeth Neeld, *Seven Choices* (Warner Books, MBI Publishing, 6706 Beauford Drive, Austin, TX 78750):222,223

"New Beginnings"

34 Ann Kaiser Sterns, Coming Back, (Random House, Inc.,1992):315

RESOURCE PAGE

For information regarding

Grieving Forward Outreach and
Educational Workshops

or to contact Linda Pouliot to
speak at your event see:

www.lindapouliot.org

or email her at

ljpouliot@msn.com

For New Hope Center for Grief Support

grief support group dates and locations

or to contact Cathy Clough to
speak at your event see:

www.newhopecenter.net

or email

griefhelp@newhopecenter.net

ORDER INFORMATION

REDEMPTION
PRESS

To order additional copies of this book, please visit
www.redemption-press.com.
Also available on Amazon.com and BarnesandNoble.com
Or by calling toll free 1-844-2REDEEM.